In this decade of destiny,
God has prophetically revealed
to Morris Cerullo the soon coming

5 MAJOR CRISES

AND

MAJOR WAVES

OF THE HOLY SPIRIT

COMING IN THE 1990's

By
Morris Cerullo

1st Printing 1990
2nd Printing 1992
Copyright © 1990
Morris Cerullo World Evangelism
Printed in the United States of America

Table Of Contents

The Decade Of Destiny

We are on the brink of spiritual destiny! One thing that God has made very clear to me is that we must draw on every truth of revelation God has been teaching us through the years. Now is the time to bring all of those truths into divine focus. It has become more important as we enter what we call this "Decade of the '90s," the Decade of Destiny.

The **key** to spiritual breakthrough is spiritual timing. Knowing what time it is...being in step with God. Not being behind Him...not running out in front of Him, but actually walking in step with Him.

The question is, what cycle are we in? The Spirit of God has taught us for many years that the cycle we are in is the **Harvest Time Cycle**!

People are talking about us coming into a harvest. We have been in a harvest time. The Church of Jesus Christ around the world has been in a harvest time cycle. But it is not just any harvest time. Harvests are also periods of time in which events take place. This harvest time is a very special time. We have had harvests in the manifestation of the move of God in days gone by. But there came a period of time when we entered into this harvest time, which is different than any other harvest time that we may have experienced as we went through the various cycles of God from the time of Jesus Christ to our modern day. This harvest time is distinguished by two things: One, it is **God's end-time harvest time.**

What distinguishes this harvest is that the culmination of this cycle will conclude with a very important event that will take place, and that event is this...Jesus is coming!

God Gave Me A Revelation Concerning This Decade Of Destiny!

In September of 1989, I made my first trip to minister to the Australian people. Theresa and I had just left Perth and were in Sydney, where we were staying overnight to catch the next plane to return to the United States. We were tired from the crusade and had arrived at our room in Sydney at about 4:00 or 5:00 o'clock in the afternoon...Mama and I. We decided we'd just take a little rest before we went out for dinner. We got into bed.

God said, "Morris, get up!" I got up from my bed, I went into the next room, and He said, "Write." And He showed to me **Five Major Crises** that are coming in the 1990s...Five Major Crises!

I wrote them down. When God gave me the message, He gave it to me specifically to plant that seed in the Body of Christ.

God showed me something else: He showed me **Five Tremendous Major Waves Of The Holy Spirit** that are coming in the nineties.

God's people are coming under a great spirit of deception, of the devil's doctrine that is permeating the Church. One of the great crises that we are going to face in this decade is a new onslaught of satanic power that is coming against the Church of Jesus Christ...where doctrines of the devil will be loosed inside the so-called Church, and multitudes of God's people in this last day will be deceived.

Some people believe we are getting this earth ready for Jesus, and that Jesus is going to come back to this earth when we build all these beautiful buildings, all these Christian schools and when we've got everything under control. That is a doctrine spread by the devil.

If you want to have this earth, you can have it. But I've got news for you. I want a "new" heaven and a "new" earth – that is where I want to live eternally.

If you don't believe there is a spirit of deception that is going to manifest itself, look at the Christian magazines, the Christian television programs and Christian television and radio stations that are giving an opportunity to those people to propagate their doctrine to the Christian communities. They are presenting these deceptive doctrines under the premise that they must present all kinds of views. That means we must present the views of the New Age people. Who says so? We've got to preach the Gospel and Christ crucified, and we have no other word to preach!

Jesus is coming! He's coming...He's coming! You and I are going to be raptured to meet Him.

In this endtime harvest, we are coming into a time of...

1. Fulfillment
2. Manifestation
3. Consummation
4. Preparation
5. Demonstration

During the Decade of the Nineties...God's time of Destiny...we will see the fulfillment of all things.

We will see the manifestation of the fullness of the power of God.

It will be a time of consummation, when God will consummate all things and wrap them up in Jesus Christ. It will be a time of preparation.

And lastly, but not least...it will be a time when we will see the greatest demonstration of the power of God that the world has ever seen!

God Has Given Us A Seven-Fold Prophecy!

Before we go any further, and move into the Crises and the Five Waves...I want to give you a seven-fold prophecy of the endtime.

Remember, the true test of every prophet of God is: what he speaks will come to pass.

Most true prophets–not self-made prophets–but most true prophets will be able to be extremely specific...not generalize. Most true prophets will be able to tell you the times, the seasons, when, where, why and how.

Look at Matthew 24:32-34: *"Now learn a parable of the fig tree; When his branch is yet tender, and putteth forth leaves, ye know that summer is nigh: So, likewise ye, when ye see all these things, know that it is near, even at the doors. Verily I say unto you, This generation shall not pass, till all these things be fulfilled."*

Paul told the Ephesians: *"Making known to us the mystery (secret) of His will–of His plan, of His purpose (And it is this:) In accordance with His good pleasure (His merciful intention) which He had previously purposed and set forth in Him, (He planned) for the maturity of the times and the climax of the ages to unify all things and head them up and consummate them in Christ (both) things in heaven and things on the earth"* (Ephesians 1:9-10, TAB).

It's God's wind-up time! Test the prophet.

When God's **fullness of time** comes, it doesn't take God long to do something. I have prophesied that Russia and all of Europe will open. I have stood on the steps of the Royal Albert Hall auditorium for 18 years in succession, in London, England, and prophesied that a great revival was coming to Europe.

Today we are on the verge of a release of God's power in all of Europe...unprecedented!

I was in Poland during the time of martial law several years ago, ministering to the ministers and preaching in the churches. I came back home and, in the midst of martial

With the destruction of the Berlin Wall and the Iron Curtain, Gorbachev was warmly welcomed in a recent visit to Bonn.

law, stood on the platform and prophesied the Communist government would fall, Poland would be free, and the Gospel would be preached in Poland.

Morris Cerullo is absolutely nothing!

I am not trying to vindicate a man, because I said this it happened...no! The glory belongs to God, because it is God Who spoke it.

We are on the brink of spiritual destiny!

Here is a seven-fold prophecy God has given us. Let me put it into your spirit before we go any further:

Prophecy No. 1

God is going to restore the five-fold ministry to the Body of Christ, and we will see His purposes fulfilled.

When Lech Walesa was starting to position the Solidarity in the early '80s, I prophesied that Poland would be **free!**

Prophecy No. 2

The true Body of Christ will rise up in the greatest demonstration of the miracle power of God we have ever experienced!

Prophecy No. 3

We are going to see and experience an endtime outpouring of the Holy Spirit. Remember Joel 2:28 to 32. That promise of the endtime outpouring only started in the Upper room. It wasn't fulfilled in the Upper Room...when God said, *"It shall come to pass...I will pour out of my spirit upon all flesh."*

Prophecy No. 4

You will go into places of worship–I won't call them church buildings – because that Church structure will be shaken. The denominational structure will be shaken. The charismatic structure of the Church will be shaken.

You will gather in places, where for days and weeks you will be living under heavenly manna, where the Holy Spirit will just flow like a mighty river. You will know – no man will be in charge – because you will know that it is a sovereign, divine manifestation that only can come from God, because the most unusual miracles will take place.

They will not just be miracles of healing...they will be supernatural acts...miracles...that can only be attributed to the God of Abraham, Isaac, Jacob...the God of Israel...the God of our fathers...the God of our Savior, Jesus Christ!

Prophecy No. 5

The Gospel will be proclaimed to the four corners of the earth...let the devil hear that until every nation, every tongue, every tribe will hear the message that Jesus is Who He claims to be – the Son of the living God!

They will not get a watered-down version of the Gospel, they will hear how Christ was placed in the grave, but the grave couldn't hold Him...death couldn't swallow Him...chains couldn't bind Him...bars couldn't hold Him... up from the grave He arose!

Jesus said this would be one of the signs of the endtimes.

Look at *Matthew 24:14: "This gospel of the kingdom shall be preached in all the world for a witness..."*

Do you know what the witness of the Gospel is? It's the fact that the grave could not hold Him. It's the fact that death could not swallow Him up. It's the fact that He tore the bars away...that He arose...that He lives! That is the witness of the Gospel...the resurrection power of our Lord!

Prophecy No. 6

Multitudes of every nationality and race will be won into the kingdom of God.

Prophecy No. 7

You won't have to look for miracles! Because creative miracles will be manifested. They will take place on an unprecedented scale. Limbs, eyes, ears...will be recreated.

You say, "Brother Cerullo, I've never heard of anything like this before." You've never been in the endtimes before!

The Father also showed me something else by Revelation...Five Waves of the Holy Spirit that are coming in the 1990s in this Decade of Destiny.

Before I go into these five crises and the five waves, I want to put something very deep into your spirit...God's endtime **strategy**! Remember that the God that you and I serve is a God of plan...He is a God of purpose...He is a God of design...and He is a God of objectivity.

Nothing will happen in this decade by accident. When you read your newspapers...when you see events taking place, don't think things are just happening. Remember, the devil is not in control...God is in control!

God has a strategy for the Church. Read I Thessalonians, chapter 5, verses 1-6, in the Amplified version; it gives us a clearer understanding of the original Greek: *"But as to the suitable times and the precise seasons and dates, brethren, you have no necessity for anything being written to you. For you yourselves know perfectly well that the day of the Lord('s return) will come (as unexpectedly and suddenly) as a thief in the night..."*

This third verse will be fulfilled within the next three years: *"When people are saying, All is well and secure, and, There is peace and safety..."*

The whole world will be lulled into a complacency, where they will feel that political unity has finally come and there is worldwide peace and safety. *"...then in a moment unforeseen destruction (ruin and death) will come upon them as suddenly as labor pains come upon a woman with child; and they shall by no means escape, for there will be no escape. But you are not in (given up to the power of) darkness, brethren, for that day to overtake you by surprise like a thief. For you are all sons of light and sons of the day; we do not belong either to the night or to the darkness. Accordingly then, let us not sleep, as the rest do, but let us keep wide awake..."*

Alert!

Watch!

Cautious!

On guard!

Put it in your spirit. God is giving a new call to the Church...an endtime strategy! Keep those five words that He has given us in your spirit. This is...

...a time of **fulfillment**

...a time of **manifestation**
...a time of **consummation**
...a time of **preparation**
...a time of **demonstration**

"Let us keep wide awake (alert, watchful, cautious and on our guard) and let us be sober (calm, collected and circumspect)" (I Thessalonians 5:1-6).

A New Endtime Call Is Coming To The Church!

There are four basic fundamental truths that we have to know if we are going to enter into God's endtime strategy. Those four things are:

1. We must know that we are God's people of Destiny!
2. We must know that we are living in the final countdown!
3. We must know that we have already entered into this time of crisis!
4. We must know that we have nothing to fear and that we are going to be 100 percent victorious!

We have to know! The strength of our position is in what we know. We have to know!

Looking at the dark clouds...looking at the circumstances...looking at the conditions – it doesn't make any difference...we have to know. Looking at all the things the devil is going to throw at the Church in this hour...it doesn't make any difference...we have to know in God's endtime strategy that we are 100 percent – not 80, not 70, not 60, not 50, not 99 percent – but 100 percent victorious and the devil is completely crushed under our feet!

There is no circumstance...there is no trial...there is no temptation...there is no persecution...no test that Satan can bring into your life that can defeat you!

There is a new call coming to the Church. In the *14th chapter* of the Gospel of *St. Mark*, beginning in *verse 32*, Jesus came to Gethsemane and He said to His disciples: *"Sit ye here, while I shall pray. And he taketh with him Peter and James and John, and began to be sore amazed, and to be very heavy; And saith unto them, My soul is exceeding sorrowful unto death: tarry ye here, and watch. And he went forward a little, and fell on the ground, and prayed...take away this cup from me: nevertheless not what I will, but what thou wilt"* (Mark 14:32-36).

Now look at the 37th verse: *"And he cometh, and findeth them sleeping, and saith unto Peter, Simon, sleepest thou? Couldst not thou watch one hour?"*

He came back and found Peter, James and John asleep.

"Therefore let us not sleep..." We cannot imagine these disciples at this critical moment with the Master, sleeping. If it could happen here, what do you think the possibilities are for the Church of Jesus Christ in these endtimes before the second coming of our Lord, slumbering and sleeping?

There is a call...a new call that is coming from God to the Church, and that call is this: Shake yourself! Take hold of yourself...shake yourself out of sleep and apathy, and rise up in these closing hours!

First, the time has come we must rise up with a new sense of purpose.

Secondly, we must rise up with a new sense of urgency!

Thirdly, we must rise up with a new sense of spiritual consecration to fulfill all that God has planned in the consummation of the endtimes. It won't happen to you unless you are determined to be a pillar.

One thing that God has done through this ministry is that He has helped us to reinterpret what a "minister" is. He is not one who puts a clerical garb on, or has a card in his pocket that he is an ordained minister of a certain denomination. That is not God's interpretation of a minister.

A minister is not somebody who has gone to Bible school or has taken three, four or five years in a theological seminary or a Bible institute and has come out and said, "I am a Bible school graduate – now I am a minister."

It is written that God has set in the Church apostles, prophets, evangelists, pastors and teachers...the five-fold ministry for the purpose of perfecting of the saints (*Ephesians 4:11*). For the divine purpose – not so the saints might come to church every Sunday morning like you do, and sit in church like a bump on a log! Everything happens right around the pulpit and right around one or two little individuals, and the rest of us just come like spectators. But the message is catching on — it is going out. Preachers are beginning to see it like never before.

It's time for us to make a new consecration, a new determination that everything that God has planned for our lives will come to pass. It is time for us to shake ourselves!

When God gives revelation, it is so that we will not only accept it, but when He gives revelation it is also specifically for the purpose that we will act on it!

It Is Time For The Church To Shake Itself Out Of Slumber!

We are a very distinct people. Our lot...my lot...your lot...in this hour is a lot different than the Christians who have gone on before us. **Don't look back!**

We're different! This is a distinct day. We are a distinct people! Do you know why? We have been given the responsibility...it is a privilege, but it is also a responsibility...to live during the age where we will see the consummation of all things...we will see **God's Endtime Plan of Destiny** come to pass before our eyes. We are a distinct people. There are no people like us. There never has been, and there never will be!

There is a powerful endtime strategy God has revealed to me that we must begin using now. It has a purpose. It has an objective...so that we can be strong...so that we can be victorious in the days to come. Jesus said: *"Be on your guard (constantly alert) and watch and pray, for you do not know when the time will come. It is like a man (already) going on a journey; when he leaves home he puts his servants in charge, each with his particular task, and he gives orders to the doorkeeper to be constantly alert and on the watch" (Mark 13:33-34, TAB).*

Now look at the next two verses. Jesus said: *"Therefore watch, give strict attention, be cautious and alert for you do not know when the Master of the house is coming, in the evening, or at midnight, or at cock crowing, or in the morning. (Watch, I say) lest He come suddenly and unexpectedly and find you asleep" (Mark 13:35-36, TAB).*

It's time for the Church of Jesus Christ to shake itself out of slumber!

Look carefully at what Jesus said in *verse 37*: *"And what I say to you I say to everybody: (Give strict attention, be cautious, active, alert and) watch!"*

God Is Calling You To Set A Watch!

The endtime strategy...the new call that God has given to the Church at the beginning of this Decade Of Destiny is to take your position at the place of the watch!

Shake yourself! Be alert! Be on guard! Come to strict attention! This isn't something in which you and I have a choice. In the original Greek translation, Jesus is saying, "Keep a sharp lookout! Don't sleep." We have no choice. He is not giving us an either/or. He is giving us a command. He is saying, *"I say this to you and I say this to everybody."*

Now let's look at *verses 35-37* in the Living Bible:

"Keep a sharp lookout! For you do not know when I will come, at evening, at midnight, early dawn, or late daybreak. Don't let me find you sleeping. Watch for my return..." (Mark 13:35-37, TLB).

Now look at these last words which are the command of Jesus: *"This is my message to you and to everyone else." This is what I am commanding you to do. This is my message to you....watch! Set yourself! Be alert! Be on guard!"*

This is my message to you and to everyone else! The message and the strategy of God to the Church for this hour is this: **Set a watch!**

All truth is parallel!

There are soldiers who are assigned the special duty to guard...to stand watch. They guard the barracks...they guard the command post. The watch is set for around the clock. It is set for 24 hours a day, and under no circumstance or condition...regardless of what may happen...is that soldier allowed to leave his post.

The duties of this watchman are seven-fold:

1. He has to be **constantly** on the alert.

2. He must **watch** for any sign of the enemy.

3. He must **guard** the camp.

4. He must **protect** the camp.

5. He must **challenge** – he can't be passive.

6. God's soldiers must be **militant**.

We must be violent. God is teaching us that if we are going to succeed, we must rise up with that new determination to let everything that God has planned to happen in our lives come to pass. It won't happen by happenstance.

It does not matter even if a superior officer comes, if they try to enter the premises, the duty of that watchman is to confront them...stop them. If they do not have the password, and they don't stop, he shoots. It does not make any difference if they are a general...he doesn't let them get by. He does not let them get through. They must know the password.

You say, "Brother Cerullo, what is the password for God's Army?"

Jesus!

All power is given unto Me...**Jesus**!

In My Name...**Jesus**!

That is the password!

7. He must send out an **alarm and warn** of any danger.

God is going to show us a relationship that we must have with each other in this last day where we are not going to live unto ourselves. It is not our lives that are at stake. It is the life of the Body of Christ that is at stake. It is not just our family that is at stake. It is the family of God that is at stake.

You had better know how to guard, stand watch, be alert, and be ready to warn others of impending danger, because it's coming. It's coming! The danger is coming!

I've got news for you...the enemy does not have the password! When he gets as far as where the guard is, we are going to destroy him.

Those who fail to hear and obey what the Spirit of God is saying to His Church today...and those of us who fail to hear what the Spirit of God is saying to His Church in this endtime, I prophesy to you, you will fall. You will not be able to stand against what is coming.

In this 13th chapter of Mark, in these verses, again and again Jesus is saying stay alert. He is saying be on watch. He is saying keep a sharp lookout! He is saying this is My message to you.

I do not really care where you come from in your spiritual life or who you are, the time has come when we must do everything possible within our power now to prepare ourselves for the coming of the Lord.

Now!

We have been complacent. We have just been hearing people preach about the second coming. We have sat in our pews and just said, "Oh, isn't it wonderful, Jesus is coming," and "Praise God," and "Hallelujah!" We have had a good time but we have done nothing to prepare ourselves for that event.

The hour has come...the Word of the Lord is coming across to you...it is time for you to invest in your spiritual life now!

Set a watch! Shake off the sleepiness! Shake off the apathy! Shake off the lethargy! Set a watch!

Jesus said: *"Surely, I say to you, this generation (the whole multitude of people living at that one time) positively will not perish or pass away before all these things take place"* (Mark 13:30, TAB).

We've got to know that this is God's endtime.

There is a time fixed. It is in God's timetable...when God has planned for Christ to return. Things are not just happening and then suddenly God is going to decide Jesus is coming. It is fixed. There will be no vacillation. There will be no changing of this time. God knows when it is going to be. It is already fixed and we are moving toward that time.

We are commanded to watch. Look at *Mark 13:32-37*, in the King James version: *"But of that day and that hour knoweth no man, no, not the angels which are in heaven, neither the Son, but the Father. Take ye heed, watch and pray: for ye know not when the time is. For the Son of man is as a man taking a far journey, who left his house, and gave authority to his servants, and to every man his work, and commanded the porter to watch. Watch ye therefore: for ye know not when the master of the house cometh, at even, or at midnight, or at the cock crowing, or in the morning: Lest coming suddenly he find you sleeping. And what I say unto you I say unto all, Watch"* (Mark 13:32-37).

Three times...again and again and again Jesus is saying, **watch**!

Jesus said, "This is My message!" Not just to a handful of people...not just to a little select group...not just to some special people...not just to some unusually called-out individuals...but this is My message to everyone! **Watch! Be alert!** Stand on guard! Because in such an hour as you think not, the Son of man shall return.

In the original Greek, it does not mean just "watch" with your eyes...or to keep awake. It means "looking" and "expecting" something to happen. Jesus said watch, look and expect something to happen. Watch, look and expect something to happen! Watch, look and expect something to happen!

This is the Word of the Lord to you. Let it go deep down into your spirit and act on it! God has revealed His will to you. He has revealed what is coming in the decade of the nineties. Now it is your responsibility to receive it and obey. Begin to set a watch as you now read about the Five Crises and the Five Major Waves of the Holy Spirit during this Decade of Destiny!

Chapter 1

We Live In The Climax Of The Ages

As we enter the decade of the nineties, we are entering the most exciting, challenging period of time the Church has experienced since its birth. We are on the very threshold of spiritual destiny!

We are on the brink of experiencing the greatest manifestation of the power and glory of God the world has ever seen!

We are entering into a time of fulfillment; God is bringing to fruition His plan and purposes for His people. Not one promise...not one prophecy...not one word God has ever spoken through His prophets throughout the ages is going to fail.

After explaining to His disciples the signs which would be taking place upon the earth before His coming, Jesus told them: *"Now learn a parable of the fig tree; When his branch is yet tender, and putteth forth leaves, ye know that summer is nigh: So likewise ye, when ye shall see all these things, know that it is near, even at the doors. Verily I say unto you, **This generation shall not pass, till all these things be fulfilled**"* (Matthew 24:32-34).

We are the most privileged generation of God's people to ever live! Right before our eyes we are seeing prophecy after prophecy being fulfilled in God's endtime plan. I believe we are the generation that will hear the trumpet of God sound and see with our eyes Christ returning in great power and glory! Praise the Name of the living God!

We are living in the climax of the ages...a time of consummation, where God is bringing all things together and heading them up in Christ. Paul wrote to the Ephesians: *"Making known to us the mystery (secret) of His will–of His plan, of His purpose. (And it is this:) In accordance with*

His good pleasure (His merciful intention) which He had previously purposed and set forth in Him, (He planned) for the maturity of the times and the climax of the ages to unify all things and head them up and consummate them in Christ, (both) things in heaven and things on the earth" *(Ephesians 1:9-10, TAB).*

We are part of God's endtime plan! God's plan and purposes which He planned before the foundation of the earth are being fulfilled! This is a time of manifestation in which He has purposed to bring the Body of Christ into full maturity...where we have grown unto the full stature of Jesus Christ...where there is a full manifestation of God's power flowing through us with miracles, signs and wonders following. We have not yet seen this happen. But it is coming!

You and I are part of God's spiritual destiny!

God is going to restore the fivefold ministry to the Body of Christ and we are going to see His purposes fulfilled.

The true Body of Christ is going to rise up in the greatest demonstration of the miracle power of God we have ever experienced.

We are going to see and experience a great endtime outpouring of the Holy Spirit, unparalleled in history!

The Gospel is going to be proclaimed to the far corners of the earth until every nation, tongue and tribe has been reached!

Jesus said this would be one of the signs of the endtimes. He said, *"And this gospel of the kingdom shall be preached in all the world for a witness unto all nations; and then shall the end come"* *(Matthew 24:14).*

Multitudes of every nationality and race are going to be won into the Kingdom of God!

Creative miracles are going to take place on an unprecedented scale!

We are going to witness this great endtime outpouring Joel prophesied would come before the day of the Lord! Joel prophesied: *"And it shall come to pass afterward, that I will pour out my spirit upon all flesh; and your sons and your daughters shall prophesy, your old men shall dream dreams, your young men shall see visions: And also upon the servants and upon the handmaids in those days will I pour out my spirit. And I will show wonders in the heavens and in the earth, blood, and fire, and pillars of smoke. The sun shall be turned into darkness, and the moon into blood, before the great and the terrible day of the LORD come. And it shall come to pass, that whosoever shall call on the name of the LORD shall be delivered: for in mount Zion and in Jerusalem shall be deliverance, as the LORD hath said, and in the remnant whom the LORD shall call" (Joel 2:28-32).*

This prophecy was partially fulfilled on the Day of Pentecost when the Holy Spirit was poured out upon the 120 gathered in the Upper Room. But we have yet to see the great endtime outpouring of the Holy Spirit upon all flesh prior to the day of the Lord, when God has promised to manifest supernatural signs...blood, fire and pillars of smoke...signs in the heavens and earth.

Simultaneously, as God's Spirit is being poured out, God's people are going to face the greatest confrontation and assault from Satan and his demon principalities that man has ever known or experienced.

For the last two years I have been warning the Body of Christ that Satan is launching an all-out war against God's people.

We have not yet seen the full intensity of his attack. In this final endtime assault he is going to unleash his fury, his evil principalities and powers, in an attempt to destroy God's people. In John's vision of the endtimes, he saw Satan cast down to the earth and an angel cried out: *"...Woe to the inhabiters of the earth and of the sea for the devil is come down unto you, having great wrath, because he knoweth that he hath but a short time"* *(Revelation 12:12).*

We are going to see an increase in occultic and demonic activity, where demons will manifest themselves and there will be a direct confrontation with God's people.

Sin...violence...crime are going to continue to increase beyond anything we can imagine.

A wave of satanic deception is going to sweep across the world so strong that multiplied thousands will be deceived, including many so-called Christians.

As the Spirit of God is working mightily through His

people, Satan and his principalities are going to be working through his demons to hinder and stop the work of God. Satan, knowing his time is short, is going to pour out his wrath upon the Body of Christ, and we are going to experience the greatest spiritual confrontations we have ever faced. Christians who do not recognize what is happening, or do not know how to exercise spiritual authority over Satan and his demon principalities, are going to be overwhelmed, and will not be able to stand.

The '90s Are Going To Be A Time Of Final Revelation!

Our position of strength as we enter this Decade of Spiritual Destiny is in knowing and being prepared for what God is going to do. God does not want us to be groping in the dark spiritually...not knowing what He has planned...not knowing what the enemy is going to do. It is not His will that we be confused...afraid...unprepared.

From the very beginning of His dealings with the nation of Israel, God chose to reveal His plans to His people through His servants, the prophets. On Mount Sinai, God spoke through Moses, revealed His plans for them as a nation and entered into a covenant with them.

Before they entered the promised land, He again revealed His plan and purposes for them as His people. As they faced opposing armies, He spoke through His prophets and revealed the plans of their enemies...how and when they were going to attack. He spoke through His prophets to warn His people of coming judgments...of famine and drought.

While Israel was in Babylonian captivity, God rolled back the pages of time and revealed to Daniel a detailed plan concerning what He has planned for His people in the endtimes.

Think about it. More than two thousand years ago God revealed to Daniel His endtime plan which has been sealed up until now! God told Daniel, *"Go thy way, Daniel: for the words are closed up and sealed till the time of the end. Many shall be purified and made white, and tried; but the wicked shall do wickedly: and none of the wicked shall understand; **but the wise shall understand** " (Daniel 12:9-10).*

God told Daniel the "wise" shall understand. Those saints of God who are walking in close covenant relationship with Him are going to know (and understand) the signs of the times and what God is doing upon the earth.

The truths concerning the endtime have been sealed up and reserved until God's appointed time...until now. By His Spirit He has been revealing His endtime plan to us so that we will know and be prepared for what is going to happen upon the earth in this endtime harvest. These secret truths are going to remain sealed to the wicked and unbelieving. God said, *"...none of the wicked shall understand."*

We have a written account of Christ's revelation of the endtime events that are going to take place. Look at Revelation, chapter one, verse one: *"The revelation of Jesus Christ, which God gave unto him, **to show unto his servants things which must shortly come to pass**; and He sent and signified it by his angel unto his servant John" (Revelation 1:1).*

The book of Revelation is not the revelation of a man, but of Jesus Christ...the revelation which God gave Him **for the purpose of making known to His servants the things which are going to happen upon the earth at the final consummation of the ages**. God hasn't planned for you to be perplexed or fearful about the future. He has planned for you to know and understand what is going to happen.

Throughout the ages, at crucial points in the lives of His people, God spoke to them through His prophets to reveal His plan and purpose. As the children of Israel were entering a new period of time...of spiritual destiny...where they were crossing over Jordan and taking possession of the promised land, God spoke through Moses to prepare them for what they were going to face. He reminded them of God's promised blessings and warned them of the judgments of God that would come upon them for their disobedience. Moses said: *"See, I set before you today life and prosperity, death and destruction. For I command you today to love the LORD your God, to walk in his ways, and to keep his commands, decrees and laws; then you will live and increase, and the LORD your God will bless you in the land you are entering to possess. But if your heart turns away and you are not obedient, and if you are drawn away to bow down to other gods and worship them, I declare to you this day that you will certainly be destroyed. You will not live long in the land you are crossing the Jordan to enter and possess. This day I call heaven and earth as witnesses against you that I have set before you life and death, blessings and curses. Now choose life, so that you and your children may live and that you may love the LORD your God, listen to his voice, and hold fast to him. For the LORD is your life, and he will give you many years in the land he swore to give to your fathers, Abraham, Isaac and Jacob" (Deuteronomy 30:15-19, NIV).*

At another point of great spiritual destiny, before the Church was born, Christ gathered His disciples together in the Upper Room to prepare them for what they were going to face. They were about to be thrust into a time of great upheaval and uncertainty as they were entering a new spiritual dimension where they were going to be anointed and empowered as the Body of Christ to fulfill His will upon the earth. Jesus did not leave them to face the coming days of trials and opposition without preparing them to be victorious.

Jesus told them: *"I have told you all these things so that you should not be offended—taken unawares and falter, or be caused to stumble and fall away, and to keep you from being scandalized and repelled. They will put you out of the synagogues—expel you. But an hour is coming when whoever kills you will think and claim that he has offered service to God. And they will do this because they have not known the Father nor Me. But I have told you these things now so that when they occur you will remember that I told you of them" (John 16:1-4, TAB).*

Jesus prepared them beforehand for what they were going to face so they would not stumble or fall away.

He had warned them that He was going to be taken, crucified and resurrected on the third day (*Luke 9:22*). He had told them they would be hated of all men for His Name's sake...that they would be scourged and put into prison. He warned them that they would be persecuted and killed (*Matthew 24:9*). But He had also promised to pour out upon them the Holy Spirit, which would give them power and authority to overcome the power of Satan and to be His witnesses to the ends of the earth!

Jesus knew the tremendous crises they were facing which they, in their own limited natural strength, would not be able to stand. But He did not leave them to face these crises on their own. He told them He was going to send the Comforter, Who would be in them and would give them dunamis power from on high to equip them as His witnesses.

Jesus said: *"Nevertheless I tell you the truth; It is expedient for you that I go away: for if I go not away, the Comforter will not come unto you; but if I depart, I will send him unto you" (John 16:7).*

Before He ascended into heaven, He told them, *"...behold, I send the promise of my Father upon you: but tarry ye in the city of Jerusalem, until ye be endued with power from on high" (Luke 24:49).*

Just as it was necessary for the disciples to be prepared, equipped and empowered by the Holy Spirit to face the crises they were facing, the only way we are going to be able to stand and be victorious during the crises that are coming in the decade of the nineties is through the power and anointing of the Holy Spirit.

Just as God used His servants, the prophets, to warn and prepare His people for what they faced, as we enter this decade of spiritual destiny...the last decade of the twentieth century...He is going to use His servants, the prophets, today to reveal His endtime plans and prepare His people for what is coming upon the earth before Christ's return.

God intends for you to know, understand and be prepared for what is going to happen in this endtime harvest.

The prophet Amos declared, *"Surely the Lord God will do nothing without revealing His secret to His servants the prophets" (Amos 3:7, TAB).*

God still has prophets today who are being used to prepare an endtime people! God has spoken through me prophetically throughout the years in preparing and warning God's people of the events that are going to be taking place in God's endtime harvest.

"Son, tell My people that very soon everything that can be shaken will be shaken."

At that time, God began to show me the great shaking that was going to take place all over the world and in every area of life...in governments, in economies, in social structures, in doctrines, in Christian experiences, in families, in every area. In 1977, I wrote about this shaking in my book, *Revelation Healing Power.*

Soon after this book was printed, God revealed to me that this time of shaking He had shown me had already started. He showed me what was being shaken, Who was doing the shaking, why there was a shaking. I wrote about it in my book, *The Shaking Has Started.*

Early in the eighties, God gave me the harvest time revelation, showing specific things which will be happening during God's endtime harvest cycle.

The true test of a prophet is, what he speaks will come to pass. One by one we have seen these prophecies being fulfilled.

Now, God is lifting the veil of darkness from our spiritual eyes and giving us a small glimpse into what we are going to face in the coming decade of the nineties.

God has shown me Five Major Crises we are going to face as the Body of Christ. These crises are far greater than any we have ever experienced. We must not only be aware of these coming crises, we must begin to prepare ourselves so we will be fully armed and prepared to confront and defeat Satan and his principalities.

God has also revealed to me Five Major Waves of the Holy Spirit that are coming. God wants you to prepare yourself so that you will be ready and receptive as the Holy Spirit begins to move. God wants you to experience a special endtime anointing so you will rise up in the position of power and authority He has planned for you...where you have grown to full maturity...unto the full stature of Jesus Christ. He is raising up endtime people through whom He can manifest His power and glory to the world, who will be used mightily as an endtime witness in the nations of the world.

We are entering a Decade of Spiritual Destiny. However, it is up to you whether or not you experience the fullness of all that God has for you in this endtime hour. It is up to you whether or not you are going to be victorious during the crises that are coming in the nineties. It is up to you whether or not you are going to be part of this endtime move of the Holy Spirit.

The exact time and nature of events in this endtime hour were prophetically revealed to me in **The Shaking Has Started.**

Hear what the Spirit of God is saying: *"He that hath an ear to hear, let him hear what the Spirit saith" (Revelation 2:7).*
Receive it deep into your spirit.

God is Going To Manifest Himself Through A Holy Remnant!

Not everyone in the Church today is going to move in the power and manifestation of God's anointing in these final hours of time. A separation is coming. The Body of Christ is going to go through a purifying process that will separate the wheat from the chaff (*Matthew 3:12*). We are going to be tried **as gold** is tried in the fire until all the impurities...all the things in our lives which are not of God...are burned away.

The gold represents this spiritual refining process we are going to experience; you are going to be tried until you come forth as pure gold *"And he shall sit as a refiner and purifier of silver: and he shall purify the sons of Levi, and purge them* as gold *and silver, that they may offer unto the LORD an offering in righteousness" (Malachi 3:3).*

God is going to bring a **remnant**...a holy seed...through this purifying fire, who are...100 percent consecrated...100 percent committed to the work of God...100 percent dead to self! God is going to have a people!

Not everyone claiming to be a born-again Christian is going to be part of this great endtime move of God. Many are so bound by tradition, a love for the things of this world, and so caught up with self, that they will be unwilling to make the necessary dedication and consecration God requires. This is where a great separation will take place.

It is upon this remnant...this purified, holy people...the power and glory of God is going to rest. The power and Presence of the glory of God will be among His people. The prophet Zechariah prophesied, *"For I, saith the LORD, will be unto her a wall of fire round about, and will be the glory in the midst of her" (Zechariah 2:5).*

In the midst of the coming crises and the things that are coming upon the earth before Christ's return, God's power and glory will be upon His people to strengthen and make them victorious. He is going to pour out an endtime anointing upon them and use them in fulfilling His purpose of reaching every nation, tribe and tongue with the saving Gospel of Jesus Christ.

It is through these holy, anointed people He will manifest miracles, signs and wonders to the world. Everywhere they go, they will speak the Word in a demonstration of power, and God will confirm it with signs and wonders. Regardless of the opposition we will face, the Word of God will prosper and increase until the entire world is filled with the knowledge of the Lord. Habakkuk prophesied, *"For the earth shall be filled with the knowledge of the glory of the LORD, as the waters cover the sea" (Habakkuk 2:14).*

As the true Body of Christ begins to function according to God's divine structure, with the fivefold ministry functioning as God intended, the work of God around the world is going to increase at an accelerated rate, even greater than the growth of the early Church. Denominational barriers will be broken as the members of the Body of Christ begin to walk in covenant relationship with one another, united together in the Spirit for one common goal of fulfilling the divine commission of evangelizing the world.

The nineties will be a time of final preparation for the Body of Christ before Christ's return. My spirit is grieved within me and I am deeply burdened because the majority of Christians today are not spiritually strong enough to face these coming crises. The majority of Christians have fallen into a spiritual stupor or slumber. They are not aware of the lateness of the hour. They are like the servant in Jesus' parable who said, *"My lord delayeth his coming"* (*Matthew 24:48*).

The apostle Peter speaks of scoffers in the last days, walking after their own lusts, saying, *"Where is the promise of his coming? for since the fathers fell asleep, all things continue as they were from the beginning of the creation"* (*II Peter 3:4*).

We are living in the final countdown of the ages, yet the Body of Christ is not prepared. Many Christians have become lazy and indifferent, thinking they have plenty of time. They have become so caught up and entangled with the cares of this life that they are no longer watching or looking forward to Christ's coming.

While the Church has been sleeping, Satan and his demon principalities have been intensifying their efforts in preparation for this hour. It is time for us, as the Church of Jesus Christ, to shake ourselves and rise from our sleep! It is time to wake up and see that Satan and his principalities have already established demonic strongholds throughout the world through the New Age movement, the occult, Satan worship and other diabolical influences in preparation for the establishment of a new one-world order, a one-world religious system, a new worldwide economic system under a new world leader!

Satan and his demonic principalities are organized and prepared to make this final assault. Satan has strategically placed men and women in every phase of society...governments, news media, education, financial institutions, military forces...to influence and propagate his demonic doctrines.

While Satan and his demonic forces have been working feverishly to attack and destroy the Church, most Christians in our churches have not even been aware that a great spiritual battle has been growing in intensity. In many churches the members have failed to recognize or admit Satan and his demons are real and working in the world today. Pastors have been afraid or reluctant to talk about Satan and, more importantly, have failed to teach their members how to fight spiritual warfare and exercise power and authority over him and his demon forces. The Church as a whole is unprepared...unprepared to fight Satan and his demon principalities, and unprepared in this crucial hour to take their position of power and authority in fulfilling the work of evangelizing the world before Jesus comes.

Before Christ came to the earth, the great prophet, John the Baptist, was sent *"to make ready a people prepared for the Lord" (Luke 1:17)*. In this hour before Christ's second coming, He is going to use His prophets to make ready a people prepared for the Lord! As God's servant, this is my responsibility today.

Jesus said: *"But of that day and hour knoweth no man, no, not the angels of heaven, but my Father only. But as the days of Noe were, so shall also the coming of the Son of man be. For as in the days that were before the flood they were eating and drinking, marrying and giving in marriage, until the day that Noe entered into the ark,* ***And knew not until the flood came, and took them all away; so shall also the coming of the Son of man be.***" *(Matthew 24:36-39)*.

For 120 years Noah was faithful to warn the people of coming judgment. They refused to listen. They ignored his warning. They rejected the Word of the Lord spoken through him and continued to live their lives according to their own desires until the very day Noah entered the ark and the door was closed. As a result of their continual rejection and indifference to this word of warning, they were unprepared and did not know until the flood was upon them.

Jesus said, *"As the days of Noe were, so shall the coming of the Son of man be."* He warned this same spiritual condition of indifference, unconcern and unpreparedness would exist before His second coming. Today God's servants are declaring, "Jesus is coming. It's time to prepare!" But the majority of Christians continue on with "business as

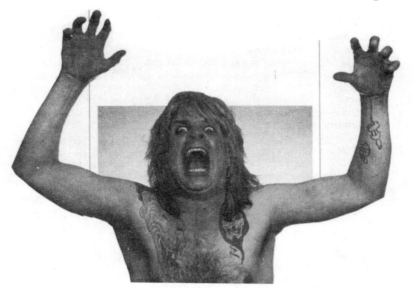

Heavy-metal singers like Ozzy Osborne employ diabolical influences in their music.

usual"...unaware of the lateness of the hour...unaware that Satan and his principalities are raging throughout the earth furiously preparing for this final hour. Don't think for one minute that Satan and his demons are sitting back wasting one minute. They are feverishly working night and day to tear down and destroy the true Church.

The Church is unprepared for what we are going to face in this endtime hour! It is time for God's people to stop arguing about when the rapture is going to take place and make final preparations for His coming.

Jesus said: "Watch therefore: *for ye know not what hour your Lord doth come. But know this, that if the goodman of the house had known in what watch the thief would come, he would have* watched, *and would not have suffered his house to be broken up. Therefore,* **be ye also ready: for in such an hour as ye think not the Son of man cometh** " (Matthew 24:42-44).

As we enter this Decade of Spiritual Destiny together,

we must be spiritually alert. God is saying to us to "set a watch in prayer!" Not only must we be on the alert, we must take action!

I must warn you, **don't take what I say lightly**. Hear what the Spirit of God is saying and move into action. Don't allow anyone or anything to hinder you from taking time to prepare.

Knowing the lateness of the hour, we must make a new consecration and dedication to God and to His work. We must rededicate everything we have...time...energy...talent...finances.

As we unite together in a closer covenant relationship with one another and with God, we must not allow anything to hinder or stop us from giving ourselves 100 percent. We cannot be halfhearted. We cannot withhold or pull back, but must increase all our efforts.

Two thousand years ago, a handful of believers...about 120, who had gathered together in the Upper Room...stood on the brink of spiritual destiny. Jesus had commissioned them to go into all the world and make disciples of all nations, and they had assembled together in one mind and one accord to receive the Holy Spirit, which would give them the power and authority to fulfill this commission.

That handful of believers was baptized in the Holy Spirit and left the Upper Room full of the power and anointing of God. *"And with great power gave the apostles witness of the resurrection of the Lord Jesus: and great grace was upon them all" (Acts 4:33).* The Word of God was preached in a mighty demonstration of power, with signs following, and multitudes were added to the Church.

They experienced phenomenal growth! Against all odds...persecution, imprisonment, beatings, torture and death...that small handful of believers multiplied until the entire world at that time was evangelized in just 200 years!

The reason they were able to accomplish what we have failed to do in 2000 years is because they were single-minded. *"Now the company of believers **was of one heart and soul**, and not one of them claimed that anything which he possessed was (exclusively) his own, but everything they had was in common and for the use of all" (Acts 4:32, TAB).*

Not only were they walking in such close covenant relationship with one another where they no longer claimed their possessions exclusively as their own, but for the use of all; they had focused all their efforts upon one common purpose...to fulfill the commission of evangelizing the world. They considered no sacrifice too great...houses, lands, family, friends, and even their own lives...for the sake of the Gospel. They did not selfishly cling to their worldly possessions or their lives, but were dedicated and consecrated unto death.

The apostle Paul suffered the loss of all things, but he considered them as dung (*Philippians 3:8*). He had his heart and mind set upon one purpose...fulfilling the work Christ had called him to do. He was single-minded...there was nothing else in his life drawing him away from this purpose. He was 100 percent sold out...dead to self! He said, *"...for I am ready not to be bound only, but also to die at Jerusalem for the name of the Lord Jesus" (Acts 21:13)*.

He was ready to endure all things...persecution...beatings...stonings...imprisonment and death. Affliction, pain, hunger, suffering did not stop him from fulfilling that purpose. He said, *"But none of these things move me, neither count I my life dear unto myself, so that I might finish my course with joy, and the ministry, which I have received of the Lord Jesus, to testify the gospel of the grace of God" (Acts 20:24)*.

Rise To A New Level Of 100 Percent Consecration To God

Today the Church of Jesus Christ is entering into a period of the greatest spiritual destiny it has ever experienced or will ever experience! We are living in the final countdown when God's endtime plan is going to be fulfilled and Christ is coming in the clouds of glory. We are going to see prophetic endtime events culminating in the end of the ages.

At this point of spiritual destiny we face a tremendous challenge. At the present time there are 5.052 billion people on the face of the earth...over half of them...2.026 billion...have never heard the Name of Jesus. If the population continues to increase at its present rate, there will be 6.127 billion people by the year 2000.

The 5 Major Crises And 5 Major Waves Of The Holy Spirit

We are not going to be able to evangelize the world and reach the billions of lost souls in the nations of the world with the current dedication and commitment of the majority of Christians today. There are too many who are so entangled with the cares of this life...they are holding onto their possessions and continually striving to obtain more instead of focusing their minds upon reaching the multitudes who are lost while there is still time.

In the years to come, when the Church faces the fiercest attack and persecution from Satan and his principalities that we have ever experienced, God is going to raise up a **remnant** of people who have totally sold out to Him...who are dedicated and consecrated unto death...who have focused all their efforts upon one common purpose...to evangelize the lost in the nations of the world.

It is this 100 percent dedication that is going to make this endtime people victorious over Satan. In a vision, John saw Satan's endtime war against God's people, but he did not see a defeated, cowering Church. He said, *"And they overcame him by the blood of the Lamb, and by the word of their testimony; **and they loved not their lives unto the death**" (Revelation 12:11).*

God is going to use men and women in this endtime harvest who are willing, like Paul and the believers in the early Church, to count all things but loss...who will love not their lives...who will lose sight of themselves and dedicate all they have and all that they are to the work of God in these closing hours of time.

Take your position as part of the holy remnant God is going to use in this endtime hour to fulfill His plan and purpose upon this earth! Make a new dedication and consecration to God, where you are 100 percent sold out to Him.

Hear what the Spirit of God is saying and act on it! Don't allow yourself to become spiritually sluggish or indifferent. Shake yourself and prepare for what is coming in the days ahead. Prepare for the coming of the Lord!

Paul told the Thessalonians: *"But of the times and the seasons, brethren, ye have no need that I write unto you. For yourselves know perfectly that the day of the Lord so cometh as a thief in the night. For when they shall say,*

Peace and safety; then sudden destruction cometh upon them, as travail upon a woman with child; and they shall not escape. But ye, brethren, are not in darkness, that that day should overtake you as a thief. Ye are all the children of light and the children of the day: we are not of the night nor of darkness. Therefore let us not sleep as do others; but let us watch and be sober " (I Thessalonians 5:1-6).

Remember that God has planned for you to be prepared and to be strong. A new strength is coming to the Body of Christ! God is pouring His dunamis strength...His very life...into our innermost beings.

In these last days, the true Body of Christ is going to walk in **a full manifestation of His power**. Jesus is not coming for a weak, anemic church. He is coming for a Church that has fully matured...a glorious Church that has been purified...without spot or blemish.

Daniel prophesied concerning the endtime saints, *"...but the people that do know their God shall be strong, and do exploits (great things)" (Daniel 11:32).* He said the people who know their God will be strong. He was not referring to those **claiming** to know God. He was referring to those who have a relationship with God...who have had a revelation of Who God is...who know Him in His fullness...who are walking in close relationship with Him... who are 100 percent consecrated and committed to Him.

God's endtime Church is not only going to be strong and victorious during the coming crises and the events that will take place before Christ's return, we are going to do exploits for God.

Not only will we be strong and immovable while everything around us is being shaken, we are going to be strong and mighty in battle as we oppose Satan and his principalities that are coming against the Church in a last-ditch effort to destroy it.

We are not going to be fearful...discouraged...defeated...running from the enemy. In the midst of the turmoil, persecution and upheaval we will face, God's people are going to do mighty exploits in battle.

In these closing hours of time, we are going to rise up in the power and anointing of Almighty God to conquer and defeat the kingdoms Satan has established in the nations of the world. We are going to become mighty in battle and put the enemy to flight!

Throughout the world men and women are going to do great spiritual exploits in establishing the work of God...in penetrating new territories such as Russia, China, Japan, and other countries that have been previously closed to the Gospel...in destroying Satan's strongholds that are hindering the work of God...in evangelizing, establishing new churches and spreading the Gospel to every corner of the earth.

Regardless of the coming crises or the opposition, trials, afflictions, persecution you may face, you can be strong, victorious and mighty in battle! The key to experiencing this strength is in being spiritually prepared and on the alert.

Chapter 2

Crisis 1: A Crisis Of Change

As we enter the decade of the nineties, God has shown me that we are going to face major crises in every area of our lives. These crises will be unlike anything we have ever experienced. People are going to be fearful and perplexed as they face problems and circumstances for which there is no natural solution.

Jesus said there would be great distress among the nations with perplexity, until men's hearts would fail them because of fear concerning the things which will be coming upon the earth.

"And there will be signs in the sun and moon and stars, and upon the earth distress (trouble and anguish) of nations in bewilderment and perplexity (that is, without resources, left wanting, embarrassed, in doubt, not knowing which way to turn) at (the echo) the roaring of the tossing of the sea; Men swooning away or expiring with fear and dread and apprehension and expectation of the things that are coming on the world; for the (very) powers of the heavens will be shaken and caused to totter. And then they will see the Son of man coming in a cloud with great (transcendent and overwhelming) power and (all His kingly) glory (majesty and splendor)" (Luke 21:25-27, TAB).

During these crises, God's hand is going to be upon His people. Those Christians who are living in covenant relationship with God and have their faith fixed upon Him and His Word will be strong and immovable. Regardless of the circumstances they face, they will be victorious!

The first major crisis God has revealed to me that is coming in the nineties is a crisis of change.

In the nineties we are going to experience such dra-

Climate of change! East and West Berlin march together in a rally for unification.

matic changes people will find it difficult to cope with them, and they are going to find themselves in a crisis situation...in a state of turmoil!

A good example of the type of dramatic changes that will take place is the recent removal of the East Berlin Wall on November 9, 1989. After 28 years of standing as a barrier between East and West Berlin, almost overnight the border was opened. Restrictions were lifted, giving the people in East Berlin freedom to cross over freely into West Berlin.

There are many more dramatic changes such as this, in boh the spiritual and natural world, that will be occurring in rapid succession. In this decade, look for these five major changes to take place.

1. Worldwide economic change!

2. Major changes within the traditional structure of the Church!

3. Increased hatred by the world toward Christianity and Christians!

4. Intense persecution to the true Church of Jesus Christ!

5. Change in weather patterns, resulting in an increase of natural disasters around the world!

Crisis Of Change 1: Worldwide Economic Upheaval

Just as the Berlin Wall was opened suddenly, without prior announcement, the coming great economic crash will take place overnight. Even though we have seen warning signals indicating great worldwide economic upheaval, it will happen suddenly, throwing the world into a crisis of economic change and turmoil. (Similarly, when the stock market plunged unexpectedly on October 19, 1987, which has been termed "Black Monday," Wall Street was thrown into confusion and turmoil.) Government leaders, financial consultants, businessmen, will be perplexed...desperately struggling to find solutions. This will be the opening for the establishment of a one-world monetary system.

Jesus warned that one of the major signs preceding His coming would be famines. He said: *"And you will hear of wars and rumors of wars; see that you are not frightened or troubled, for this must take place, but the end is not yet. For nation will rise against nation, and kingdom against kingdom, **and there will be famines** and earthquakes in place after place; All this is but the beginning, the early pains of the birth pangs, of the intolerable anguish"* (Matthew 24:6-8, TAB).

In the past decade of the eighties we have witnessed major famines in various parts of the world...Ethiopia, Bangladesh, Biafra, Mozambique and other countries...where multiplied thousands are starving to death every day. These famines are just the **beginning**...the early birth pains as a woman in travail...of the terrible anguish that is coming upon the earth before Christ's return.

Jesus revealed to John a time of worldwide economic upheaval and turmoil coming upon the earth, when it would take a day's wages to buy enough grain to make a

"Junk Bond" stocks shattered the stability of Wall Street in the late '80s, and failed savings and loans escalated the economic crisis.

loaf of bread. In a vision John saw a black horse and the rider on its back was carrying a balance. Then he heard a voice crying out, *"A quart of wheat for a denarius (a whole day's wages), and three quarts of barley for a denarius; but do not harm the oil and the wine!" (Revelation 6:6, TAB).*

What John saw is one of the major crises we are going to see take place upon the earth before Christ's return. There is coming a great financial crisis that is going to shake the entire world.

Crisis Of Change 2: The Traditional Structure Of The Church Will Be Broken!

Major changes are going to be taking place within the structure of the organized church. God is going to break man's traditional barriers that are hindering the Church from operating as He intended. Many Christians, including pastors and Christian leaders, are going to find it very difficult to accept and cope with these changes.

As the Spirit of God begins to break through the traditional structure of the Church, a separation is coming.

Pastors, Christian leaders and laymen who are bound by their traditions, man-made doctrines and the structure of their denominations, will be unwilling to accept these changes and will remain part of the dead, dry structure of the church. They will not recognize these changes as the move of God and will resist them as the true Body of Christ.

There will be a clear-cut separation between those who refuse to compromise the truth...who are 100 percent dedicated and sold out to God...from those who are uncommitted and have compromised with the world and the harlot, apostate church.

As the Church enters into a time of intense persecution, there will be a further separation as professing Christians turn away from the truth and embrace the doctrine of the one-world church to escape persecution and the trials the true Body of Christ is going to encounter.

During the time of separation, there will be those within the Church who are going to be deceived and deluded. They are going to turn away from the truth of the Gospel and accept and believe false doctrines. Paul told Timothy: *"But the (Holy) Spirit distinctly and expressly declares that in latter times some will turn away from the faith, giving attention to deluding and seducing spirits and doctrines that demons teach. Through the hypocrisy and pretensions of liars whose consciences are seared (cauterized)..." (I Timothy 4:1-2, TAB).*

He told the Thessalonians, *"Let no man deceive you by any means: for that day shall not come, except there come a falling away first, and that man of sin be revealed, the son of perdition" (II Thessalonians 2:3).*

Dramatic changes in every area of life are going to be occurring in rapid succession. During this crisis of change, **Satan's objective is to get Christians off track by trying to cause them to become overwhelmed, fearful and discouraged by these changes. Watch for it. It is coming!**

Crisis Of Change 3: Intensified Hatred Toward Christianity

One of the changes we are going to see is an increasing animosity toward Christians. As the Berlin Wall goes down in East Berlin and doors to religious freedom are opening for a short period of time in Russia, China and other Communist countries, in the United States we are going to lose more and more religious freedom.

A time of severe persecution is coming upon the Church. Christians who believe in the Word of God and speak out against sin are going to be ridiculed, hated and persecuted. Christians who take a strong stand against abortion, homosexuality, indecent and obscene movies and television programs, are going to be branded as fanatics and ostracized.

As the influence of the New Age movement continues to infiltrate our society, bringing its Eastern religions and occultic influences...promoting a one-world religion that encompasses all faiths...Christians are going to be considered a hostile force standing in the way of world unity and peace which needs to be eliminated.

Christians who believe in sin, a literal burning hell, and that Jesus Christ is the only way of salvation, are going to be criticized and persecuted.

Churches with government-funded programs and loans, who refuse to line up with their one-world view and liberal views, will be cut off.

The hostility we see today against Christianity and Christians is going to increase at a rapid rate. A time is soon coming when Christians will have to put their jobs, their homes, their families and their lives on the line for the sake of the Gospel of Jesus Christ. (In many countries this is already happening.) This will bring a separation between those who are 100 percent sold out and consecrated to God and those who compromise the Word and are unwilling to endure persecution for the sake of the Gospel.

There are Christians who think this type of persecution will never happen in the United States. It is time for the Church to wake up! Little by little we see it happening before our eyes. Prayer has been removed from our schools, but through the influence of the New Age movement many schools are now introducing Yoga and "meditation" techniques, teaching our children how to contact "spirit guides." We cannot have a Bible in our school classrooms, yet the textbooks are filled with New Age theology, Eastern mysticism and the occult. School libraries are filled with books on Satan worship and the occult. In a Christian nation, God has been taken out of our schools.

Today it is against the law to display a nativity scene during Christmas on government-owned property unless it is surrounded with secular Christmas items.

In a country that was built on a strong foundation of Christian principles and high moral standards, we have legalized the murder of millions of unborn babies each year.

Not only has homosexuality become an accepted lifestyle, there are laws continually being introduced to protect "gay rights" and legalize homosexual marriages, giving them the same legal status and benefits as married couples.

The more the Church begins to speak out and take a stand against these sins, the more we can expect to be persecuted!

Get ready for this time of intense persecution that is coming!

Crisis Of Change 4: Endtime Persecution Of The True Church

As Jesus commissioned and sent His disciples out to evangelize the cities throughout Israel, He warned them of the persecution they would face. He told them they would be hated by all men: *"And ye shall be hated of all men for my name's sake: but he that **endureth** to the end shall be saved" (Matthew 10:22).*

Circle the word "endureth" in this verse. Put it deep into your spirit. God has planned for you to endure. I will be sharing more about the type of endurance God's people must have today to face these coming crises.

When the disciples asked Jesus concerning the signs of the end and His coming, He told them there would be wars, earthquakes, pestilences *"and fearful events and great signs from heaven" (Luke 21:10-11, NIV).* Then He told them: *"But previous to all this, they will lay their hands on you **and persecute you**, turning you over to the synagogues and prisons, and you will be led away before kings and governors for My name's sake. This will be a time (an opportunity) for you to bear testimony. Resolve and settle it in your minds, not to meditate and prepare beforehand how you are to make your defense and how you will an-*

*swer; For I (Myself) will give you a mouth and such utter-
ance and wisdom as all of your foes combined will be unable to stand against or refute. You will be delivered up and
betrayed even by parents and brothers and relatives and
friends, and (some) of you they will put to death. And you
will be hated (despised) by everyone because (you bear) My
name and for its sake. **But not a hair of your head shall
perish**. By your steadfastness and patient endurance you
shall win the true life of your souls" (Luke 21:12-19, TAB).*

In the coming years there is going to be a growing, intense hatred throughout the world for Christians and the
saving Gospel of Jesus Christ. In some countries this is
already true. Some of you will be placed in prison because
of your stand for Christ and because of your commitment
to God in spreading the Gospel. Jesus said we will be betrayed by our own families and friends and some will be
killed.

This persecution Jesus warned the disciples about not
only applied to them in their day, but also applies to us
today in this endtime hour. After the establishment of the
Church, the believers experienced tremendous persecution.
They were beaten, imprisoned and killed because of their
testimony of Jesus Christ. They were tortured, beheaded,
thrown to lions, burned at the stake, and crucified.

However, in answer to the disciple's question, "*...what
shall be the sign of thy coming, and of the end of the world?*"
Jesus said a time of persecution would be one of the signs
which would take place (*Matthew 24:4-31*).

For many years we have seen persecution of Christian
believers in Communist countries. In Russia, China and
many other countries, Christians have lost their homes and
families, have been imprisoned, tortured and put to death
for the sake of the Gospel. In the years to come, we are
going to see an increase of these types of persecution on a
worldwide scale, beginning in the United States.

It is inevitable! As sin continues to increase and the true
Body of Christ begins to rise up under the unction and
power of the Holy Spirit to speak out against sin and warn
of coming judgment, we are going to be persecuted! The
very presence of God's holy remnant of people in the midst

of the darkness of evil is going to expose the sin and we are going to be hated.

On their last night together, Jesus again warned the disciples of the persecution they were going to face. First He told them He was sending them forth in the power and authority of His Name, and that whatever they asked the Father in His Name, He would do it.

He said: *"You have not chosen Me, but I have chosen you —I have appointed you, I have planted you–that you might go and bear fruit and keep on bearing; that your fruit may be lasting (that it may remain, abide); so that whatever you ask the Father in My name (as presenting all that I AM) He may give it to you. This is what I command you, that you love one another" (John 15:16-17, TAB).*

Jesus chose and ordained His disciples to go forth in the power and authority of His Name to tear down Satan's strongholds and establish His kingdom upon the earth. In taking upon themselves Christ's Name, they were identified with Him and possessed His power and authority. It was for this reason Jesus said the world would hate and persecute them.

Jesus said: *"If the world hates you, know that it hated Me before it hated you. If you belonged to the world, the world would treat you with affection and would love you as its own. But because you are not of the world–are no longer one with it–but I have chosen (selected) you out of the world, the world hates (detests) you. Remember that I told you, A servant is not greater than his master–is not superior to him. If they persecuted Me, they will also persecute you; if they kept My word and obeyed My teachings, they will also keep and obey yours. But they will do all this to you – inflict all this suffering on you–because of (your bearing) My name, and on My account, for they do not know or understand the One Who sent Me" (John 15:18-21, TAB).*

There was no question regarding whether or not they would be persecuted. Jesus told them, *"If they persecuted Me, they will persecute you."* It was a matter of fact. The world hated Jesus because through His life and the miracles He had manifested among them, He had exposed their sins and they could no longer cover them up. Just as the world

47

hated Jesus, they also hated and persecuted His disciples because through Jesus' Name they manifested the same miracle power of God that was in Him, and exposed their sins.

As Jesus was leaving them to return to the Father, He wanted them to be prepared for the persecution and opposition they were going to face. He told them: *"I have told you all these things so that you should not be offended–taken unawares and falter, or be caused to stumble and fall away, and to keep you from being scandalized and repelled. They will put you out of the synagogues–expel you. But an hour is coming when whoever kills you will think and claim that he has offered service to God"* (John 16:1-2, TAB).

We are going to be hated of all men! We are going to be persecuted! Jesus said, *"If they persecuted Me, they will also persecute you"* (John 15:20, TAB). Christ has called us out of the world and has sent us forth in His power and in His Name. As the life and miracle power of God is manifested through us in Jesus' Name, and His holiness is manifested in our lives, the world is going to hate us because their sins are going to be exposed. Paul told Timothy, *"...all that will live godly in Christ Jesus shall suffer persecution"* (II Timothy 3:12). He did not say "some." He said "all."

In these closing hours of time, as the true Body of Christ is purified and rises up as the powerful force God intended... manifesting the power and glory of God...walking in the righteousness and holiness of God...exposing the sin of the world, we are going to face a time of intense persecution.

During this time of persecution, God has not planned for us to become discouraged, afraid or defeated.

He has warned us that persecution is coming so we will not be taken by surprise. We do not need to worry about how we will respond or what we are going to do. Jesus has promised, *"I (Myself) will give you a mouth and such utterance and wisdom as all of your foes combined will be unable to stand against or refute"* (Luke 21:15, TAB).

The Body of Christ is not going to be running or hiding in fear. We are not going to be intimidated by Satan, but are going to boldly and fearlessly proclaim the Gospel in the face of persecution and death.

Jesus said, *"What I tell you in the darkness, speak in the* *light, and what you hear whispered in your ear, proclaim upon the housetops. **And do not fear** those who kill the body, but are unable to kill the soul; but rather fear Him who is able to destroy both soul and body in hell"* (Matthew 10:27-28, NAS).

God is going to have an endtime people who are fearless and mighty in battle. He is going to have men and women who will not compromise the Word of God, who will not be fearful of man or be menpleasers.

Paul said, *"As we have said before, so I say again now, if any man is preaching to you a gospel contrary to that which you received, let him be accursed. For am I now seeking the favor of men, or of God? Or am I striving to please men? If I were still striving to please man, I would not be a bond-servant of Christ"* (Galatians 1:9-10, NAS).

When persecution comes, God's power and Presence is going to be upon His people and we are not going to be defeated. He is going to make us victorious over all the power of the enemy! Regardless of the opposition or persecution we face, *"the gates of hell shall not prevail against it (the Church)"* (Matthew 16:18). In John's vision, he saw an endtime victorious, overcoming Church! *"And they overcame him by the blood of the Lamb, and by the word of their testimony, and they loved not their lives unto the death"* (Revelation 12:11).

Opposition and persecution did not stop the believers in the early Church. They did not whine or hide in a corner. Regardless of what they faced, through the power and anointing of the Holy Spirit, they continued to fearlessly proclaim the Gospel everywhere they went. Despite every attempt of Satan to stop them, the Word of God increased mightily and prevailed (*Acts 19:20*) until the entire world was evangelized!

The early Church was not afraid of persecution. They were strong and immovable and prepared to face it. Peter told the believers not to be surprised when they were persecuted, but to rejoice! He said: *"Beloved, think it not strange concerning the fiery trial which is to try you, as though some strange thing happened unto you: **But rejoice**, inasmuch as ye are partakers of Christ's sufferings; that,* *when his glory shall be revealed, ye may be glad also with exceeding joy" (I Peter 4:12-13).*

Paul was not afraid of the persecution or afflictions he faced because he knew that the power of the Holy Spirit was upon him and would make him victorious. He said: *"...Most gladly therefore will I rather glory in my infirmities, that the power of Christ may rest upon me. Therefore, I take pleasure in infirmities, in reproaches, in necessities, in persecutions, in distresses for Christ's sake: for when I am weak, then am I strong" (II Corinthians 12:9-10).*

Paul wasn't afraid to face opposition, afflictions, persecution. He said, "Let them come!" He said, "I take pleasure in them!" Why? It wasn't because he had confidence in his own strength. He knew that when he was weak, tired, ready to give up, the dunamis miracle power of God was within him and he was made strong to face anything. He knew that when his natural strength failed, there was a supernatural powerful force within him that would take over and cause him to overcome.

Don't be surprised when persecution comes for the sake of the Gospel...expect it! Be ready for it! Some of you right now are facing persecution because of the Gospel. Do not be discouraged or afraid. Rejoice because the power and anointing of God is upon you to make you victorious. Jesus warned us so we would not stumble or fall away when persecution came.

Whatever you do, don't retreat! Don't be afraid. Do not water down or compromise the message God has given you. Do not be held back by fear of what man will do or say to you. Do not be a men-pleaser. Shout it from the housetop! Regardless of the opposition or danger you may face, endure.

Regardless of the opposition and persecution we face in this endtime harvest, the true Body of Christ is going to go forth in the power and anointing of the Holy Spirit to proclaim the Gospel to the nations of the earth. Knowing persecution is coming and that through the power of the Holy Spirit that is within us we are going to overcome every attack of the enemy, we are not fearful...we are ready!

In the nineties we are going to see a crisis of change.

The 1989 San Francisco earthquake was only one of hundreds of intensified natural disasters during this last decade.

Manifold changes are going to take place in rapid succession. Change in the world's attitude toward Christians and increased persecution is only one of the changes we are going to see. We will also see dramatic signs of changes in the natural world as well.

Crisis Of Change 5: Widespread Destruction From Increased Natural Disasters

There will be dramatic changes in weather patterns, resulting in an increase of natural disasters, earthquakes, hurricanes.

Jesus warned that one of the signs of His coming would be earthquakes in different parts of the world. He said, *"And there shall be famines, and pestilences, and **earthquakes** in divers places. All of these are the beginning of sorrows (Matthew 24:7-8).* In the past decade we have seen an increase in the number and intensity of earthquakes, with earthquakes occurring in various parts of the world on a daily basis.

The recent earthquake in San Francisco, measuring 7.1 on the Richter scale, is an example of the type of destruction we will see – multiplied many times over. Sections of San Francisco were destroyed, freeways collapsed. Nine counties were declared disaster areas, with an estimated $7-10 billion in damages. There were at least 67 confirmed deaths and 3,258 confirmed injuries.

The earthquake of 1965 in Mexico, measuring 8.1 on the Richter scale, which devastated parts of Mexico and killed an estimated 25,000, is another example of the widespread destruction we are going to continue to see.

In addition to the destruction as a result of earthquakes, in the next decade there will be an increase in the number and intensity of other natural disasters, such as tornadoes, floods, hurricanes.

Due to the "greenhouse effect," which is the slow rising of the earth's temperatures, scientists are predicting major changes in the earth's climate. The "greenhouse effect" is caused primarily by the accumulation of carbon dioxide and methane in the atmosphere, which, like the glass of a greenhouse, traps heat.

We have already experienced a twenty percent increase in carbon dioxide, which has raised temperatures about one degree fahrenheit. A change in just three degrees would make the earth the warmest it has been in 6,000 years.

This global warming will result in a change in weather patterns, as well as an increase in hurricanes, tornadoes and other natural disasters. Meteorologists are predicting more intense hurricanes in the Atlantic region in the next decade than in the '70s and '80s.

Hurricane Gilbert in 1988, which left a wide path of devastation across Jamaica and the Mexican Yucatan, was the most powerful hurricane on record in the Western Hemisphere. Its winds reached 200 miles per hour.

Hurricane Hugo, in September of 1989, ripped through the Virgin Islands, Puerto Rico, and ravaged the coastline of South Carolina, leaving 28 dead and many injured and homeless. Twelve counties in South Carolina were declared federal disaster areas by President Bush.

Meteorologists predict that due to global warming, hurricanes are going to be more powerful than any yet recorded. A rise in tropic ocean-surface temperatures will accelerate winds to 225-230 miles per hour. The wind's destructive force will go up 40 percent!

As these natural disasters...earthquakes, tornados, hurricanes...increase, we will see widespread devastation in various parts of the world. Multitudes of people will be homeless, hungry, afraid, perplexed...not knowing what to do.

Christians will experience such dramatic changes...on their jobs...family circumstances...finances...physically... that unless they are prepared, they will become fearful, unable to cope and unable to release their faith to receive what they need from God.

In the natural, any time there is a major change or crisis, it temporarily immobilizes people. It demands a tremendous amount of spiritual energy in prayer, seeking God's direction, and drawing upon Him for strength to overcome. When these dramatic changes come suddenly and quickly, Satan's strategy is to wear us down and keep us so overwhelmed we will not be aware of the lateness of the hour and will be diverted from fulfilling the work God has given us to do.

Knowing we are going to face these changes in this coming decade of the nineties, we must be watching for them so we will not be caught off guard and unprepared.

Ask God to give you a fresh revelation of the lateness of the hour in which we are now living. Regardless of the obstacles or hindrances you may face, make every effort to share the Gospel of Jesus Christ everywhere you go. Walk in a new boldness.

The time has come when God's people must sense an urgency and spiritual destiny as we double all our efforts in prayer, witnessing, giving and fulfilling the work God has given us to do. This is not a time for God's people to hold back, but to do great exploits for God!

Chapter 3

Crisis 2: The Crisis Of The Family

The one crisis that is going to have such a devastating effect upon the world is in the family.

God has shown me...

A Major Crisis Of The Family Is Coming
We are going to reap a whirlwind of rebellion, promiscuity and the breakdown of moral standards.

As we look at the growing problems families are facing today...divorce...child abuse...abortion...battered women ...teenage suicides...runaways...teenage promiscuity and pregnancy...drug, alcohol abuse...you might wonder, "How could it possibly grow worse?"

The murdering of unborn children is only one of the many sins our society is reaping on the family.

In the past twenty years, we have seen a tremendous attack upon the family. Satan has been using every possible strategy to tear down and destroy families. We are in a life and death struggle for our families! Satan has been infiltrating our homes, attacking the minds of our children, sowing seeds of violence, rebellion and sexual permissiveness. He has been sowing seeds of division, resentment, unforgiveness, to destroy marriages and family relationships.

Over the past four decades Satan has been tearing down the structure of the family and now, as we enter the nineties, we must be prepared and equipped to face an even greater onslaught of the enemy as we near the climax of the ages and the coming of Jesus Christ.

Families today are facing crises in drastic proportions!

If it were possible for me to come into your home and have a heart-to-heart talk with you and pray with you about the battles and heartaches you are facing, no doubt you would have an urgent family need or problem. I receive hundreds of letters from partners who are facing crisis situations involving their families.

I wish I could tell you that the problems and crises families are facing today are going to decrease. They are not! God has shown me that during this last decade of the century the crises we are facing are going to continue to **increase**, along with the added pressures of worldwide economic and political upheaval, until there is a major crisis of the family.

The conditions that exist in the world today...violence...crime...drugs...rape...murder...are going to grow worse as Satan and his demons unleash their fury upon this earth. These stressful conditions are going to place added pressures upon families, and many will be unable to cope with them. Jesus said that in the days before His coming sin would abound. He said, "...*And because iniquity shall abound, the love of many shall wax cold*" (Matthew 24:12).

The word "abound" is translated from the Greek word, "plethuno," which means "shall be multiplied." Gross wickedness and sin are going to cover the earth. Sin is going to be multiplied. Think for a moment about the depravity and sin that exists today...then multiply it a thousand times. That is the condition that will exist upon the earth before Christ returns. Because of this overwhelming evil, the love of many people is going to grow cold. People will become calloused and indifferent toward human suffering and to the needs of others.

Paul warned Timothy: *"But understand this, that in the last days there will set in perilous times of great stress and trouble hard to deal with and hard to bear. For people will be lovers of self and (utterly) self-centered, lovers of money and aroused by an inordinate (greedy) desire for wealth, proud and arrogant and contemptuous boasters. They will be abusive (blasphemous, scoffers)* disobedient to parents, *ungrateful, unholy and profane. (They will be) without natural (human) affection (callous and inhuman), relentless–admitting of no truce or appeasement. (They will be) slanderers–false accusers, trouble makers; intemperate and loose in morals and conduct; uncontrolled and fierce, haters of good. (They will be) treacherous (betrayers), rash (and) inflated with self-conceit. (They will be) lovers of sensual pleasures and vain amusements more than and rather than lovers of God"* (II Timothy 3:1-4, TAB).

In this evil environment, there is going to be a tremendous rebellion of young people toward their parents and toward all authority. Even young children will have a defiant attitude toward their parents.

Paul told Timothy in Verse 2 above, *"They will be abusive (blasphemous, scoffers)* **disobedient to parents**, *ungrateful, unholy and profane."*

We are going to begin to reap a whirlwind of sexual permissiveness and breakdown of moral standards. Today one-half of America's teens are sexually active. That number will continue to increase, as will the number of teenage pregnancies, AIDS and other sexually transmitted diseases. Domestic violence and child abuse will continue to grow worse.

Hosea prophesied concerning a whirlwind of destruction that would come upon Israel because of the evil they had sown. He said, *"For they have sown the wind, and they shall reap the whirlwind..."* (Hosea 8:7). Just as the nation of Israel reaped a whirlwind of destruction, the United States and all the nations who have sown seeds of corruption, sexual permissiveness, perversion and immorality are going to reap a whirlwind of pain, heartache and destruction in the family.

It is inevitable God has set forth a spiritual law that cannot be broken. Paul told the Galatians, *"Be not deceived; God is not mocked: for whatsoever a man soweth, that shall he also reap.* **For he that soweth to his flesh shall of the flesh reap corruption;** *but he that soweth to the Spirit shall of the Spirit reap life everlasting" (Galatians 6:7-8).*

Paul told Timothy that in the last days *"...evil men and seducers shall wax worse and worse, deceiving, and being deceived" (II Timothy 3:13).* He said they would be *"loose in morals and conduct, uncontrolled and fierce, haters of good" (II Timothy 3:3, TAB).* He said there would be those who continually refused to acknowledge and believe in God whom He would turn over to a **reprobate** mind (*Romans 1:28*).

Paul said: *"For they exchanged the truth of God for a lie, and worshiped and served the creature rather than the Creator, who is blessed forever. Amen. For this reason God gave them over to degrading passions; for their women exchanged the natural function for that which is unnatural, and in the same way also the men abandoned the natural function of the woman and burned in their desire toward one another, men with men committing indecent acts and receiving in their own persons the due penalty of their error. And just as they did not see fit to acknowledge God any longer, God gave them over to a depraved mind, to do those things which are not proper, being filled with all unrighteousness, wickedness, greed, evil; full of envy, murder, strife, deceit, malice; they are gossips, slanderers, haters of God, insolent, arrogant, boastful, inventors of evil, disobedient to parents, without understanding, untrustworthy, unloving, unmerciful;* **and although they know the ordinance of God, that those who practice such things are worthy of death, they not only do the same, but also give hearty approval to those who practice them"** (*Romans 1:25-32, NAS*).

This describes the immorality we see today. Not only are there people who are practicing these things, they approve, encourage and applaud others who do them.

In the coming decade of the nineties we are going to reap a whirlwind of destruction from the seeds of immorality and sexual permissiveness which have been sown and propagated throughout our society. Christian parents who have compromised their standards and have failed to establish and uphold high moral standards with their children are going to reap the tragic results.

Because of the selfishness that is going to be so prevalent and the continued high divorce rate, more and more men and women will be unwilling to make a lasting commitment to marriage and will prefer a promiscuous lifestyle. They will be concerned only with the gratification of their sexual desires.

All of these things will continue to tear at the very foundation of the family. In this immoral, wicked environment, the pressures and stress are going to come crushing down upon the family with such intensity that many families will be torn apart. Parents will be unable to cope with their rebellious children. With the increase of immorality, marriage will no longer be considered a sacred union between a man and woman. There will be a general attitude that anything is acceptable, including infidelity, sex with many different partners and homosexuality.

You may be wondering, "How are we going to be able to cope?" In an environment where men are "haters of good," who deny God and the existence of sin and have a hatred of Christians with their high moral standards, how are Christians going to keep their families strong?

During these last days before Christ comes, it is the people who know their God who will be strong! Those who know and are prepared for what is coming...who recognize how the enemy is working...who know how to exercise power and authority over Satan and his principalities... are going to be able to endure and be victorious.

The root cause of the problems families are plagued with today...divorce...promiscuity...abortion...rebellion...child abuse...infidelity...is sin. The following statistics reflect the ever-increasing results of sin:

Teenage suicides – There has been a 300 percent increase in the past 20 years.

Divorce – One out of every two marriages ends in divorce.

Child abuse – more than doubled from the decade of the seventies to the eighties.

Sexual promiscuity – The number of unwed mothers jumped 367 percent from the decade of the seventies to the eighties.

Drug abuse – has reached epidemic proportions. The percentage of youngsters beginning marijuana use in the 9th grade or earlier almost doubled over the last five years.

Abortion – Since 1973, more than 18 million unborn babies have been legally aborted in the United States. Every day in the United States, 4,100 innocent babies are murdered in their mothers' wombs. It is reported that 80 percent of that number involve teenagers.

As sin multiplies upon the earth, the crises families are facing today will also increase.

The closer we get to the second coming of Jesus, the dividing line between good and evil, God's elect and those who belong to Satan, is going to be clearly seen. This division will be so great it will create a spiritual division among family members.

Jesus warned His disciples concerning this. He told them: *"Think not that I am come to send peace on earth: I came not to send peace, but a sword. For I am come to set a man at variance against his father and the daughter against her mother and the daughter-in-law against her mother-in-law. **And a man's foes shall be they of his own household.** He that loveth father or mother more than me is not worthy of me: and he that loveth son or daughter more than me is not worthy of me" (Matthew 10:34-37).*

Jesus said that a man's enemies would be members of his own family. Why? The division Jesus was referring to in these verses is a **spiritual division** that comes because of the truth of the Gospel. Those who accept Christ and the truth of the Gospel are "set at variance" against those who refuse or reject the truth of the Gospel. The word "variance" in this verse means "to cut apart...to divide in two."

This spiritual division is at the very root of the problems

families are facing today. In families where there are members who are unsaved, there is a spiritual division...where the unsaved members are in opposition to those who are saved. This is the reason many times Christians feel much closer to their brothers and sisters in the Lord than they do to their own flesh and blood relatives.

Before Christ's coming, this spiritual division is going to be so strong it will transcend the bond of flesh and blood. There will come a time when the members of our families are either going to accept Christ or they will continue to reject the truth and turn their backs on God until they fall under the deception and control of Satan. A man's enemies will be members of his own household. Those who are under Satan's control will turn on the family members who are Christians.

Jesus said: *"Brother will deliver up brother to death, and the father his child, and children will take a stand against their parents, and will have them put to death; And you will be hated by all for My name's sake. But he who perseveres and **endures** to the end will be saved (from spiritual disease and death in the world to come)" (Matthew 10:21-22, TAB).*

Families today need to stop trying to deal with their problems without going deep down to the root cause. When you face problems in your family, you must remember you are in a spiritual battle. If you have a husband or wife who has an alcohol or drug problem, don't try to cope or deal with the problems related to alcohol or drugs. Go to the root of the problem and pray for their salvation. If you are having marital problems and your mate is unsaved, the root of your problem is spiritual division and you need to spend time in prayer and intercession for their salvation, not the surface problems.

If you are having problems with your rebellious children, the root of the problem is spiritual division. Bind the rebellious spirits and if they are unsaved, pray and intercede for their salvation.

The time has come for the Body of Christ to unite together in bringing in a harvest of unsaved loved ones while there is still time. It is time for us to step out in faith to claim the salvation of our family members and loved ones we have been praying and believing God to save for many years.

The devil has lied to us long enough! God has bound Himself to us with His Word. It's time to break the bonds Satan has put upon their lives...to remove the spiritual blindness that is keeping them from receiving Christ. It is time for us to break the deception and lies that Satan has planted in their minds!

Our position of strength as we face this coming crisis of the family is going to be in standing in the gap for our families in prayer until they are 100 percent united together with us in the Spirit...delivered and set free from Satan's bondages.

Just as the families of the Israelites were protected from the angel of death during the Passover by applying the blood of the sacrificial lamb to the doorposts of their homes, our families who are gathered together under the protection of the blood of Jesus are going to be saved from destruction!

Your position of strength during this coming crisis of the family is in knowing and being prepared for what is coming. Families will face crises in the following areas:

1. A growing spiritual division where unsaved members will be in opposition to those who are saved. This will cause increased turmoil within families and unless Christians recognize what is happening, Satan will use family problems to wear them out, drain their spiritual energy and hinder them from walking in the victory God has planned in this endtime hour. This spiritual division will become so intense children will take a stand against their parents, parents will turn against their children and brother will turn against brother (*Matthew 10:21-22*).

2. There will be an ever-increasing breakdown of moral standards; **not only acceptance but a promotion of a promiscuous lifestyle**, opening a floodgate of infidelity, incest, pedophilia, multiple partners, homosexuality, bestiality and every possible evil perversion. As a result of this increase of immorality, families are going to reap the tragic results...teenage pregnancies, abortion and divorce (*Romans 1:28-32*).

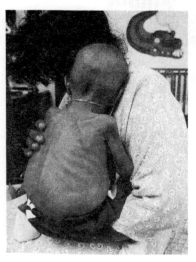

This innocent baby is now dying from AIDS – a plague in our society that is the direct result of sexual sins.

3. There will be a continued increase in AIDS and other sexually transmitted diseases (*Romans 1:26-27*).

4. Domestic violence, incest and child abuse will continue to grow worse.

5. A spirit of rebellion and defiance will take hold and young people will rebel against their parents and all authority (*Romans 1:30*).

6. There will be an increase in teenage suicides, as more and more young people are unable to cope with the pressures they are facing...drugs...gang violence... sexual promiscuity...and family problems such as broken relationships with their parents, lack of parental love and support, the breakup of their families through divorce.

7. Families will experience severe problems in their relationships due to the added pressure of a worldwide economic crisis. There will be an intense financial struggle to provide for their basic necessities such as food, clothing and shelter, particularly for single-parent families.

8. As the "traditional" family unit...father, mother and children...continues to deteriorate through the world's promiscuous lifestyle and divorce, marriages are going to face a greater assault than ever before as Satan continues to attempt to destroy the sanctity of marriage and the home.

9. The very foundation of the family unit will continue to be torn apart through the infiltration of humanism and the New Age philosophies (with its Eastern religions) that are being taught in our schools.

10. Through the influence of television, Satan is going to continue to tear down and destroy the moral values and Christian standards which once formed a solid foundation for our families. Programs on major networks featuring sexual permissiveness, adultery and fornication will continually grow worse, with scenes of nudity, sexual intercourse and homosexual relationships.

Chapter 4

Crisis 3:
The Shaking Of The Church

We are going to experience a major crisis in the Church that is going to change the structure of the Church as we know it today. The true Body of Christ is going to emerge and take on a new form.

For years God has been speaking prophetically through me that we are going to see radical changes taking place within the structure of the Church. The true Church of Jesus Christ is going to emerge out of the dry, lifeless shell of man's organization as the fully mature, powerful force God intended for it to be.

Here are the five major ways the Church will encounter crises:

1. Intense persecution on a worldwide scale, beginning in the United States.

2. Separation of the true Body of Christ from the uncommitted, compromising so-called Christians. During this separation there will be those who turn away from the faith because they have listened to seducing, lying spirits, and because they are unwilling to endure persecution for the Gospel.

3. The traditional structure of the Church that has been established according to man's organization will be shaken. The ministry of the Church will no longer revolve around the role of the pastor working under a denominational structure. Out of this dead, dry structure will arise the true Body of Christ, who will begin to function under the leadership of the fivefold ministry.

4. New leadership within the fivefold ministry will emerge, who will function under the Divine Headship of Jesus Christ and will lead a remnant...the true Body

of Christ...into fulfilling the spiritual destiny God has ordained for it in this endtime harvest.

5. Traditions and man-made doctrines are going to be broken. Members of the true Body of Christ are going to break free from their traditions, look beyond denominational barriers and come into a unity of the Spirit where they are one body...working together toward one common goal of evangelizing the world.

The vast majority of Christians today have a very limited concept of the Church. To many, the Church is limited to the four walls of the building we call the "church" or to a specific denomination. To others it has become a social club, an institution, and, in some of the larger churches, it has become a well-organized business.

The Church of Jesus Christ is not a building! It is not a denomination! It is not an organization that has been established through man's knowledge or ability.

God never intended for the Church to become an "organization." A legal definition of an organization is "an administrative, functional structure, characterized on the complete conformity to the standards of man."

God has not planned for the structure to be based upon the standards or the requirements of what man may ask of us. The Church is a living, breathing organism, comprised of multitudes of thousands upon thousands of believers all over the world. It is a living supernatural organism. An "organism" is defined as "a comprehensive, living system of intertwined parts."

The Church is not a product of man. It is God's creation. He breathed His very life into it over two thousand years ago. On the day of Pentecost, He brought it into existence and infused it with His divine life...by the supernatural power of the Holy Spirit! His intention was that it be a living organism composed of many different members who are all interdependent. Paul said, *"For as in one physical body we have many parts (organs, members) and all of these parts do not have the same function or use, so we, numerous as we are, are one body in Christ, the Messiah, and individually we are parts one of another–mutually dependent on one another" (Romans 12:4-5, TAB).*

We are all members of one body, with Christ as the divine Head and supreme authority over the Church. We are to function as His Body, in complete submission and obedience to Him. Not only did Christ purchase the Church with His own blood, God established Him as Head of the Church and gave Him a position of authority over all things.

Jesus Christ is seated today *"Far above all principality, and power, and might, and dominion, and every name that is named, not only in this world, but also in that which is to come: And hath put all things under his feet, **and gave him to be the head over all things to the church, which is his body, the fulness of him that filleth all in all**"* (Ephesians 1:21-23).

The Church Today Is Disjointed

Now, for a moment let us take an honest look at the structure of what we call the Church today. Instead of being one Body in Christ, every member mutually dependent upon the other, with Christ as our Head, the Church has become disjointed, with many organizations and denominations that are separated by traditions and doctrines of men.

These church organizations and denominations are governed by an executive committee or council, who have the overall responsibility of providing leadership for the entire denomination under this authority. There are regional or state overseers, bishops under their authority, reporting to them, who provide leadership on a statewide or regional level.

These organizations are further broken down, with a district pastor providing leadership to the local pastors of congregations. On a local church level, the pastor and church board or board of deacons are the "head" or governing authority over the local church.

Within this man-made structure, 95 percent of the ministry of the church revolves around the leadership of the pastor. God never intended for the major responsibility for leadership within the Body of Christ to be relegated just to local pastors. Yet that is what has happened today. The Church, as a whole, looks to and depends upon pastors working under a denominational structure as their major source of leadership.

When Christ ascended into heaven, He established the fivefold ministry as His divine structure for the Body of Christ, with Him as the Head. Look at the *Amplified version of Ephesians, Chapter Four, verses 11-13: "And His gifts were (varied; He Himself appointed and gave men to us,) some to be apostles (special messengers), some prophets (inspired preachers and expounders) some evangelists (preachers of the Gospel, traveling missionaries), some pastors (shepherds of His flock) and teachers. His intention was the perfecting and the full equipping of the saints (His consecrated people), (that they should do) the work of ministering toward building up Christ's body (the church). (That it might develop) until we all attain oneness in the faith and in the comprehension of the full and accurate knowledge of the Son of God; that (we might arrive) at really mature manhood, the completeness of personality which is nothing less than the standard height of Christ's own perfection – the measure of the stature of the fullness of the Christ, and the completeness found in Him."*

God has ordained that the Body of Christ function under the leadership of the fivefold ministry of the apostles, prophets, evangelists, pastors and teachers. There are those within the church today who claim that the ministry of the apostles and prophets have ceased...that they are no longer necessary...that they were only used to establish the Church. There is not one verse of scripture in the Bible that substantiates this.

The Word says God has established the fivefold ministry until we all...the Body of Christ...grow unto full maturity unto the full stature of Jesus Christ!

God has not changed the structure of His Church. Man has tried to substitute a structure of his own and, as a result, has failed miserably to accomplish His purpose of bringing the Church to full maturity.

In the next few years a crisis is coming to the traditional church that is going to shake this man-made structure to its foundations. Man-made traditions and denominational barriers are going to break and crumble and the fivefold ministry is going to be restored to the Church. The ministry of the true apostles and prophets is going to be recognized within the Body of Christ, and will begin to function once again as God intended. I am not referring to the self-appointed prophets and apostles, but to those who have been called and ordained by God.

The emphasis of church leadership will no longer be centered around the ministry of the pastor. Neither will the ministry of the Body of Christ be limited to the ministry behind the pulpit or revolve around the ministry of the pastor of the local churches. God's people are going to break free from the tradition that has held them back, and they are going to rise up under the leadership of the fivefold ministry to do the work of the ministry.

When the early Church was established, the apostles appointed elders or pastors whose responsibility was to oversee and care for the churches. This was their basic function. The three titles of elder, presbyter and bishop in the New Testament will refer to the same ministry office of the pastor. The Greek word for "pastor" is "poimen," which means "a shepherd," one who tends herds or flocks (not merely one who feeds them).

God never intended for pastors to control or rule over their congregation with an iron hand. There are pastors today who are so afraid of losing their members, they exercise strict control over their members to keep them in line with their way of thinking. There are some who are actually afraid and jealous when their members begin to move out in the power of God, manifesting signs and wonders, and they try to bring them under their control and stop the moving of the Spirit. Manipulation from the pulpit is going to stop!

The true Body of Christ will no longer be bound by or depend upon the denominational structure of men for leadership. Christ is going to be recognized as the Head of the Church and we will begin to look to the men and women of God who are functioning within the fivefold ministry under the leadership of Christ.

Members of the Body of Christ will begin to look beyond denominational barriers and come into a unity of the Spirit where they are working together toward one common goal of evangelizing the world.

Jesus prayed, *"That they all may be one, as thou, Father, art in me, and I in thee, that they also may be one in us: that the world may believe that thou hast sent me" (John 17:21)*. This unity in the Spirit will come after there is first a separation of the true from the false...between those professing Christians and the true Body of Christ.

Members of the true Body of Christ will no longer consider themselves simply as members of a particular denomination or church organization, but will enter into a new covenant relationship with one another, where they recognize themselves as members of one body...the Body of Christ.

During this crisis God is going to break down man's traditional ideas and concepts concerning the operation and function of the Church. There will be a great resistance by many to these changes. There will be many pastors, ministers and church leaders who will reject and oppose the changes in the structure of the Church, because they have built themselves little kingdoms and they will be afraid of losing the control they have over their members and the financial support.

Many pastors, ministers, church leaders and laymen will be so bound by their traditions and man-made doctrines, they will be unable to recognize or accept the move of the Holy Spirit as God begins to restore the fivefold ministry to the Church and bring it to full maturity. Their traditions and denominational structures will blind them from seeing the endtime moving of the Holy Spirit and the restoration of the Church.

There will be a clear-cut distinction in the Body of Christ between those who refuse to let go of their traditions and manmade doctrines and those who have set their minds to follow the leading of the Holy Spirit and be part of the endtime move of God regardless of the personal cost to them. Out of the dead, dry, traditional structure of the church is going to rise up a remnant...a holy seed...who are going to make up the fully mature, victorious, glorious Church of the living God!

When the children of Israel entered into the promised land and took possession of it, there was only a remnant of those who were delivered out of Egyptian bondage who entered and took possession of the land. Out of 2 1/2 million, only two...Joshua and Caleb...and the younger generation born during the 40 years in the wilderness inherited the land. Why? Because they believed God's promises and regardless of the opposition they faced, were 100 percent sold out, ready to follow God. Talk about persecution...the entire congregation of the Israelites was ready to stone them, along with Moses and Aaron, and set up new leadership that would take them back to Egypt!

Joshua and Caleb took possession of the promised land because they were 100 percent consecrated to God and were willing to let go of everything to obey God. The 2 1/2 million Israelites, including Moses and Aaron, did not enter into the promised land, because of their unbelief and rebellion (*Numbers 20:12-29*).

God told them: *"Doubtless ye shall not come into the land, concerning which I sware to make you dwell therein, save Caleb the son of Jephunneh and Joshua the son of Nun" (Numbers 14:30).*

A remnant under the new leadership of Joshua crossed over Jordan and took possession of their inheritance.

A remnant out of the dead, dry, traditional form of the Jewish nation broke free and emerged to form the Church and take possession of the kingdom of God. One hundred twenty men and women...who were 100 percent consecrated to God...who were ready to follow God regardless of the cost...came out of the Upper Room under a divine, supernatural power and anointing to fulfill a divine mandate.

The Holy Spirit swept through the nation of Israel, breaking down man's traditions and the wall separating the Jews and Gentiles, and a remnant...a new nation emerged called the people of God.

Paul said concerning the prophecy God spoke through Hosea concerning His remnant: *"Just as He says in Hosea, Those who were not My people I will call My people, and her who was not beloved (I will call) My beloved. And it shall be in the very place where it was said to them, You are not My people, they shall be called sons of the living God. And Isaiah calls out (solemnly cries aloud) over Israel: Though the number of the sons of Israel be as the sand of the sea, **only the**

remnant, *a small part of them, will be saved (from perdition, condemnation, judgment)!" (Romans 9:25-27, TAB).*

Paul said, *"For he will finish the work, and cut it short in righteousness: because a short work will the Lord make upon the earth" (Romans 9:28).*

We who were not a nation...who were once not called the people of God...are now a holy seed...sons of the living God!

Just as God raised up a remnant out of the dead, dry traditions of the nation of Israel, in this endtime harvest the Spirit of God is going to sweep through the organized structure of the church, breaking down traditions and denominational barriers to raise up a remnant...a holy seed... to fulfill His purposes upon this earth and take their position as the pure and spotless Bride of Christ who will rule and reign with Him forever!

We Must Break Free Of The Traditions Of Men!

God is raising up new leadership within the fivefold ministry under His divine authority who are going to build up the Body of Christ and lead this holy remnant into fulfilling the spiritual destiny God has ordained for it!

Man-made traditions and doctrines are going to be broken! To be part of this remnant, men and women are going to have to be willing to break free from their traditions and, like Joshua and Caleb, be 100 percent consecrated in obeying God and following the leading of the Holy Spirit.

The Pharisees and scribes came to Jesus asking why His disciples refused to stay within their religious structure and keep the tradition of the elders.

Jesus called them hypocrites and condemned them for holding onto their traditions and thereby rejecting the commandments of God. He told them: *"... Well hath Esaias prophesied of you hypocrites, as it is written, This people honoureth me with their lips, but their heart is far from me. Howbeit in vain do they worship me, **teaching for doctrines the commandments of men.** For laying aside the commandment of God, ye hold the **tradition of men**, as the washing of pots and cups: and many other such like things ye do. And he said unto them, Full well ye reject the* *commandment of God that ye may keep your own tradition...Making the word of God of none effect through your tradition, which ye have delivered..." (Mark 7:6-9,13).*

Within the structure of the Church today, there are many who, like the religious leadership of the Pharisees and scribes, are actually rejecting God's Word and rejecting the move of the Holy Spirit because of their unwillingness to let go of their own traditions and man-made doctrines.

Their traditions are nullifying the Word of God in their lives and are keeping them from taking possession of all that God has provided for them in His covenant with them. These traditions and denominational barriers are hindering the Body of Christ from functioning together as one Body, manifesting the power and glory of God to the world.

Are you willing to let go of the traditions and man-made doctrines and follow the Holy Spirit in 100 percent consecration to God and the fulfillment of His will upon the earth? That is what it is going to take if you want to be part of this endtime remnant God is raising up as the true Body of Christ.

The Body of Christ...God's holy remnant...is going to go through four phases as it breaks out of the dead, traditional structure of the church:

1. Repentance
2. Separation and Consecration
3. Holiness
4. Restitution, Restoration

As we prepare for Christ's coming, we must hear what the Spirit of God is saying and act on it. Christ's message to the Church today is "repent!" Before the Body of Christ can rise up in a full manifestation of the Holy Spirit to bring in a great harvest of souls, we must come to a place of true repentance.

Over and over in Christ's message to the churches, He calls them to repentance. To the Church in Ephesus who had lost their first love, Jesus said: *"...**Repent**, and do the first works; or else I will come unto thee quickly, and will remove thy candlestick out of his place, **except thou repent** " (Revelation 2:5).*

To the Church in Pergamos, who had allowed compromise to enter the Church, Christ warned: *"**Repent**; or else I will come unto thee quickly, and will fight against them with the sword of my mouth" (Revelation 2:16)*.

To the Church in Thyatira, who had allowed false doctrine and idol worship into the Church, He warned: *"Behold, I will cast her into a bed, and them that commit adultery with her into great tribulation, **except they repent of their deeds**" (Revelation 2:22)*.

To the halfhearted, dead, dry, formal church in Sardis, Jesus warned: *"Remember therefore how thou hast received and heard, and hold fast, and **repent**" (Revelation 3:3)*.

To the lukewarm, self-satisfied church in Laodicea, Jesus warned: *"So then because thou art lukewarm, and neither cold nor hot, I will spew thee out of my mouth...as many as I love, I rebuke and chasten: **be zealous therefore, and repent**" (Revelation 3:16,19)*.

All of these conditions are present in the Church today. Christ is calling us to repentance. It is repentance or judgment.

Following this time of repentance, there is going to come a time of separation. Those who have separated themselves from the world, who have made a 100 percent consecration, who want to be part of a holy remnant of people, are going to be separated from the sideline compromisers and those who are unwilling to let go of their traditions and man-made doctrines.

After this separation will come a move of the Holy Spirit, bringing an endtime remnant into an experience of true holiness, restitution and restoration.

Chapter 5

Crisis 4:
A Worldwide Financial Crisis

We are on the verge of experiencing one of the greatest crises we have ever experienced that is going to shake the world, plunging it into a state of great turmoil and perplexity! God has shown me...

**A Major Financial Crisis Of Worldwide
Consequence Is Coming!**

We are going to experience a worldwide economic upheaval resulting in the collapse of our monetary system. This economic crash will come suddenly, sending shockwaves throughout the world. It will be the opening for the establishment of a new one-world monetary system under a new one-world government.

Every day we move closer toward this worldwide economic upheaval and disaster. In 1980, I shared in my book *The Shaking Has Started* what God had shown me about a coming financial disaster:

"There is beginning a worldwide economic shake-up such as there has never been before in the history of the world. It will accelerate quickly.

"The finest minds in the country today are at work on financial matters in an effort to stabilize our economy. There will come a time when the economists will think that they have their problems licked...but disaster is going to come like a whirlwind. Only those with fixed faith will escape the dire consequences of the greatest economic shake-up ever to hit our nation. It will make the Wall Street crash seem like a picnic."

I warned my partners of this at the beginning of the

The failed savings and loan crisis is only a small portion of the world-wide economic chaos we will see in the next decade.

eighties. Today, as we enter the decade of the nineties, worldwide inflation will continue to soar.

The value of the U.S. dollar will continue to steadily decrease.

The national debt has reached a staggering figure in the trillions! American IOUs outstanding are actually 25 percent greater than the official figure which has increased six-fold since 1968 to $2.1 trillion.

The number of bank failures has nearly quadrupled since 1983, as economic conditions continue to force more and more banks into bankruptcy. In 1987, 184 banks closed, with 17 more kept open only by federal assistance.

In February of 1989, more than 500 thrift, savings and loan associations were bankrupt and President Bush inaugurated a $123 billion plan to bail them out. According to the *U.S. News and World Report,* 700 of the 2,950 savings and loan associations now taking deposits are bankrupt. Experts are predicting that within a decade the number of savings and loan associations will shrink sharply to as few as 1,000.

On "Black Monday" (October 19, 1987), unexpectedly the stock market plunged to its lowest point since the Wall Street crash of 1929. Wall Street was thrown into confusion and turmoil. This 1987 plunge was only a small indicator of the great financial disaster that is just over the horizon.

Every nation on earth today faces great financial instability and growing economic failure, with seemingly no hope in sight.

Worldwide economic disaster is coming! It will come like a whirlwind, throwing the world into a state of panic. How are we, as God's people, going to cope during this financial crisis?

Following the great economic crash in 1929, there was mass hysteria on Wall Street...fear...panic...a sinking feeling of desperation, as thousands of people were bankrupt overnight. Unable to cope with their financial losses, many people turned to suicide.

When this worldwide economic disaster hits, it will be unlike anything we have ever experienced. The world will be thrown into a state of shock. Panic and fear will grip the hearts of people everywhere. They will be confused, not knowing what to do or where to look for help.

As the world struggles desperately to survive this financial disaster, those Christians who are living in a close covenant relationship with God will not be fearful or shaken. In the midst of this financial upheaval and turmoil, God's hand of supernatural provision is going to be upon His people. There will be a divine sufficiency, and God's people will be strong and their needs will be met!

Daniel prophesied, *"The people that do know their God shall be strong and do exploits!"* (Daniel 11:32).

Satan Is Sitting On The Finances Of God's People!

Our position of strength, as we enter the decade of the nineties knowing we are going to face this great financial crisis, is not going to be based upon how much money we are able to store up in our savings account. It is not going to be based upon stocks, bonds or real estate investments. The day is coming when none of these things will mean anything. Our position of strength is going to be based upon our entering into a covenant of blessing and prosperity with God.

God's will for His people during this endtime harvest is not only that we be debt-free...not only that we have our own needs supplied...but that we also have the finances we need to fulfill the ministry God has given us of covering the earth with the Gospel of Jesus Christ!

Several months ago God revealed to me that Satan has a stranglehold on the finances of God's people. Many of you are now facing a severe financial crisis. Your bills have continued to pile up and there isn't enough money coming in to meet your monthly commitments or to provide for the basic needs of you and your family.

It is time for us to raise our level of faith and break Satan's hold on our finances. The devil is a liar!

It is not God's will that you be lacking!

It is not God's will that you be in debt!

It is not God's will that you scrape bottom each month to make ends meet!

It is not God's will that you worry or be fearful about how you are going to pay your bills, put food on the table and care for your family!

It is not God's will that you do not have enough money to give to the work of God!

It is not God's will that the work of God be hindered for a lack of finances!

Satan is sitting on the finances of God's people! Many of you are deeply in debt and in the natural there seems to be little hope of ever getting out. The only way you are going to break his hold and take what God has already provided for you in His covenant with you is to know and act in faith on His Covenant of Blessing and Prosperity.

The time has come for God's people to get their eyes off the natural...off themselves...off their paychecks...and get them on a supernatural God Who stands ready to supernaturally provide for their needs!

God is going to shake the economy of the world so strongly that we are going to have to get back to knowing that it is He Who provides our daily bread. We are going to have to know that *"man shall not live by bread alone, but by every word of God" (Luke 4:4).* Those Christians who are trusting in themselves, who have not learned to look to God and trust Him for their daily provision, will not be able to stand.

This coming crisis will be a time of testing the faith of God's people, to see if they will remain faithful to Him.

Those who have placed their faith and trust in the things of this world...in their bank accounts, in their own ability to provide for themselves and their families...will be shaken.

During this time, the people of God will be clearly distinguished from the world by God's supernatural provision in their lives. It will not be the **absence** of problems and adversity among God's people that will be a witness to the world, but in the midst of this financial crisis the world is going to see God's strong arm of provision for His people.

God's plan and purpose has always been to bless and prosper His people! For 430 years the Israelites were slaves under cruel Egyptian bondage. They lived in abject poverty and want. They toiled under the hands of hard taskmasters. But when God supernaturally delivered them out of the hands of the Egyptians, there was not one feeble person among them and He brought them forth with the riches of Egypt. Not only did He deliver them out of the bondage under the Egyptians, He delivered them out of their bondage of poverty!

*"He brought them forth also with silver and gold: and there was not one feeble person among their tribes. Egypt was glad when they departed: for the fear of them fell upon them. He spread a cloud for a covering; and fire to give light in the night. The people asked, and he brought quails, and **satisfied** them with the bread of heaven. He opened the rock, and the waters gushed out; they ran in the dry places like a river. For he remembered his holy promise, and Abraham his servant. And he brought forth his people with*

joy, and his chosen with gladness: And gave them the lands of the heathen: and they inherited the labor of the people" (Psalm 105:37-44).

God gave them the spoils of Egypt. *"And the LORD gave the people favor in the sight of the Egyptians, so that they lent unto them such things as they required. **And they spoiled the Egyptians** " (Exodus 12:36).*

God delivered them out of their poverty. From the very beginning He blessed and prospered them until they had an abundance of everything they needed. To give you an idea of the wealth they carried out of Egypt, later when Moses asked for a freewill offering to build the tabernacle, they gave 29 talents and 730 shekels of gold, which was over one ton of gold! The silver was 100 talents plus 1,775 shekels, which weighed a little over three and three-quarter tons! The bronze was 70 talents and 2,400 shekels, which weighed about two and-one-half tons!

On Mt. Sinai, God entered into a covenant of blessing and prosperity with Israel that was based upon their obedience.

God promised to bless them above all the nations of the earth!

"If you fully obey the LORD your God and carefully follow all his commands I give you today, the LORD your God will set you high above all the nations on earth" (Deuteronomy 28:1, NIV).

God promised to command His blessing upon all that they put their hand to!

The LORD will command the blessing upon you in your barns and in all that you put your hand to, and He will bless you in the land which the LORD your God gives you" (Deuteronomy 28:8, NAS).

God promised to give them superabundance and prosperity!

And the Lord shall make you have a surplus of prosperity, through the fruit of your body, of your livestock, and of your ground, in the land which the Lord swore to your fathers to give you" (Deuteronomy 28:11, TAB).

God promised to open His storehouse and pour out such a blessing upon them that they would never have to borrow money!

The LORD will open for you His good storehouse, the heavens, to give rain to your land in its season and to bless all the work of your hand; and you shall lend to many nations, but you shall not borrow" (Deuteronomy 28:12, NAS).

God promised the Israelites that all of these blessings would follow after them and overtake them...they would literally run after them and take hold of them...if they obeyed Him.

Through their forty years of wandering in the wilderness, God supernaturally provided for them and all their needs were met. He rained manna down from heaven and opened the rock and caused water to gush forth. In forty years their clothes and shoes did not wear out.

When He brought a **remnant** of Israel into the promised land, He caused them to inherit great cities, houses they did not build that were full of things they did not labor for, wells they had not dug, vineyards and olive trees which they had not planted (*Deuteronomy 6:10-11*). He promised to bring them into a land where there would be no shortage of food and they would lack nothing (*Deuteronomy 8:9*).

God has not changed!

It is His will today to bless and prosper His people just as He did Israel. We are God's spiritual Israel and these very same promises of blessings and prosperity belong to us today.

God has entered into a Covenant of Blessing and Prosperity with us, just as He did with Israel. Within this covenant, He has made provision for us that all...not some, but all...our needs be met. He has provided salvation, healing, deliverance, forgiveness of sins, and has promised to bless and prosper us. There are many Christians today who accept by faith God's provision of salvation and healing but do not accept God's provision for their finances.

Every promise He made to the children of Israel belongs to us!

Just as He delivered Israel out of the bondage of poverty, He has delivered us out of the bondage of poverty. Poverty brings bondage. It brings suffering. It places heavy burdens upon people that are hard to bear. It hinders people from getting their needs met. It robs

God's people of the greatest joy we can have of giving to God and His work.

He has forever broken the bondage of poverty and has made it possible for His people today to inherit the wealth of the land. The devil is a liar! The wealth of this world does not belong to the wicked; it belongs to God! God spoke through the prophet Haggai: *"...I will shake all nations,* **and the desire and the precious things of all nations shall come in, and I will fill this house with splendor**, *says the Lord of hosts. The silver is Mine, and the gold is Mine, says the Lord of hosts" (Haggai 2:7-8, TAB).*

There is no shortage in the house of God! All the wealth of the world...the gold, silver, diamonds, precious jewels, natural resources...belong to God and He has planned for us to take possession of them, just as Israel took the spoils of Egypt and took possession of the wealth God had given them in the promised land!

God is going to shake the nations and cause the wealth of the world to come to His endtime remnant!

Israel broke their covenant with God. They disobeyed and rebelled against Him. Only a remnant...two men *"who followed God fully"* and the younger generation born in the wilderness...entered in and inherited the land with its wealth! When they entered the promised land, Moses warned them not to forget that it was God Who had prospered them, satisfied every need, multiplied their gold and silver and all that they had.

He warned: *"And beware lest you say in your (mind and) heart, My power and the might of my hand have gotten me this wealth. But you shall (earnestly) remember the Lord your God;* **for it is He Who gives you power to get wealth, that He may establish His covenant which He swore to your fathers, as at this day"** *(Deuteronomy 8:17-18, TAB).*

Israel entered in and took possession of the land and all the wealth God had promised them. They took possession of houses, lands, gold and silver. It did not belong to the wicked...it belonged to God's people! God drove out their enemies and gave them the "spoils" of the wicked. In *II Chronicles, chapter 20*, Jehoshaphat and the Israelites had so much spoils from the victory of their battle they could not carry it all. It took them three days to gather it up and carry it away!

"And when Jehoshaphat and his people came to take their spoil, they found much among them, including goods, garments, and valuable things which they took for themselves, **more than they could carry.** *And they were three days taking the spoil because there was so much"* (II Chronicles 20:25, NAS).

How would you like to have a blessing unlike any other blessing...one that would be so great you could not carry it?

Are you beginning to see the picture? God had entered into a Covenant of Blessing and Prosperity with Israel. It was He Who gave them the power...the ability...wisdom... talent...to get wealth!

God Has Entered Into A Covenant Of Blessing And Prosperity With Us

The nation of Israel soon forgot God and forfeited the blessings because of their continued rebellion and disobedience. Instead of reaping the blessings and prosperity of God, they reaped the curses. Read them in *Deuteronomy 28:45-60.* The heavens were closed to them. Instead of reaping an abundance of crops, there was drought and the locusts and palmerworm destroyed their crops. Their enemies dispossessed them and they were scattered to the far corners of the earth.

But God promised a time of restoration when He would raise up a remnant of people who would again reap an abundance of His blessings.

God promised through Isaiah: *"And I will bring forth a* **seed** *out of Jacob, and out of Judah an inheritor of my mountains: and mine* **elect** *shall inherit it, and my servants shall dwell there"* (Isaiah 65:9).

Because Israel continually rejected God and disobeyed Him, they forfeited their inheritance. But God promised to raise up a seed. He promised to give them a new name. He told the Israelites who had turned their backs on Him, *"You will leave your name to my chosen ones as a curse; the Sovereign LORD will put you to death, but to his servants he will give another name"* (Isaiah 65:15, NIV).

It is this seed...His elect...that are going to take hold of His inheritance of the wealth of the land.

"We are that holy seed...that endtime remnant that He has chosen and called from the nations of the earth to be His people! We who were once not called the people of God are now a holy seed...the sons of the living God! (Romans 9:26-27).

God has entered into a Covenant of Blessing and Prosperity with us that is an everlasting covenant and He is going to cause **us** to inherit the wealth of the nations! The wealth of the wicked truly is laid up for the just (*Proverbs 13:22*). The wealth of the world does not belong to the wicked; it belongs to God and it is He Who gives us the power to get wealth!

God promised concerning this time of restoration:

*"And I will restore to you the years the locust hath eaten, the cankerworm, and the caterpillar, and the palmerworm, my great army which I sent among you. **And ye shall eat in plenty, and be satisfied** and praise the name of the LORD your God, that hath dealt wondrously with you: and my people shall never be ashamed. And ye shall know that I am in the midst of Israel, and that I am the LORD your God, and none else: and my people shall never be ashamed" (Joel 2:25-27).*

God has promised that we will eat in plenty and be satisfied!

God has promised us that in this time of restoration we will eat the wealth of the nations Isaiah prophesied: *"They will rebuild the ancient ruins and restore the places long devastated; they will renew the ruined cities that have been devastated for generations. Aliens will shepherd your flocks; foreigners will work your fields and vineyards. **And you will be called priests of the LORD, you will be named ministers of our God. You will feed on the wealth of nations and in their riches you will boast.** Instead of their shame **my people will receive a double portion**, and instead of disgrace they will rejoice in their inheritance; and so they will inherit a double portion in their land and everlasting joy will be theirs" (Isaiah 61:4-7, NIV).*

God said we will feed on the wealth of the nations. He said we will inherit a double portion!

How would you like to receive a blessing unlike any other blessing...inherit a double portion of what Israel had?

Why haven't we in the Body of Christ today taken possession of God's promises of blessing and prosperity?

We haven't taken possession of our inheritance for the same reason Israel forfeited theirs...because of our unbelief and disobedience!

Israel broke their covenant and forgot God:

"They kept not the covenant of God, and refused to walk in his law; And forgat his works, and his wonders that he had shown them" (Psalm 78:10-11).

Israel was filled with unbelief: *"...They believed not in God, and trusted not in his salvation:" (Psalm 78:22).*

Israel limited God: *"Yea, they turned back and tempted God, **and limited the Holy One of Israel. They remembered not his hand, nor the day when he delivered them from the enemy.***

Like Israel, we have forgotten that it is God Who gives us the power to get wealth. He cannot go contrary to His word and bless that which we ourselves have cursed. We've been looking to man. We've been depending upon ourselves instead of looking to God and acting on His promises. Through our unbelief we have limited the holy One of Israel!

God has promised to bless and prosper us above the nations of the earth so that we would not have to borrow. What have we done? Instead of believing and acting on God's Covenant of Blessing and Prosperity...instead of believing and trusting God for His supernatural provision... we have depended upon the arm of flesh. We have looked to man...to our paycheck...to the bank...to the credit card companies.

God does not want us to depend upon man's methods in getting our needs met. He wants us to depend upon Him as our source. The banks and lending institutions are not the answer.

It is not God's will for us to exist on borrowed money, or to have credit cards as a quick "fix" to our financial problems. God wants us to remember and **know** that it is He Who gives us power to get wealth. God wants us to quit limiting Him, believe His promises of blessing and prosperity, obey and act in faith on what He has promised.

How would you like to receive a blessing unlike any other blessing...one that would be so great you would not have enough room to contain it?

In His Covenant of Blessing and Prosperity with us, He has promised to open the windows of heaven and pour out His blessings in such abundance that we will not have enough room for it: He has promised to rebuke the devourer! *"Bring ye all the tithes into the storehouse, that there may be meat in mine house, and prove me now herewith, saith the LORD of hosts, if I will not open you the windows of heaven, and pour you out a blessing, that there shall not be room enough to receive it. And I will rebuke the devourer for your sakes..."* (Malachi 3:10-11).

Are you facing a financial crisis in your life? Is Satan binding your finances where you do not have the money you need to meet your needs? God says "Prove Me!" As you give to Him, He will rebuke the devourer...He will break Satan's hold on your finances and supernaturally meet your need.

In His Covenant of Blessing and Prosperity, He has promised that when we honor Him with our substance... with the wealth He has placed in our hands...He will bless us with plenty...the greatest possible abundance.

Honor the LORD with thy substance, and with the first-fruits of all thine increase: So shall thy barns be filled with **plenty**, *and thy presses shall burst out with new wine"* (Proverbs 3:9).

The word "plenty" in this verse means "fullness; abundance." The Hebrew root word is "to become satisfied." The expression "so shall thy barns be filled with plenty" depicts the greatest possible abundance. God wants you to enjoy plenty...He wants you to be satisfied...to have all your needs met. I am not saying that all of God's people are going to drive Cadillacs or have million dollar homes, but that His blessings are going to be upon them and they will have all their needs met!

In His Covenant of Blessing and Prosperity, He has promised that if we praise Him and pay our vows, He will deliver us in time of trouble. *"Offer to God the sacrifice of thanks-giving; and pay your vows to the Most High, And call on Me in the day of trouble; I will deliver you and you shall honor and glorify Me" (Psalm 50:14-15, TAB).*

When we keep our covenant with God and are faithful and obedient to His Word in paying our vows and giving our tithes and offerings, we do not need to beg or plead with God. He said, "Just call and I will answer." He has promised us, *"...before they call, I will answer; and while they are yet speaking, I will hear" (Isaiah 65:24).* He said that in times of trouble...in the midst of the financial difficulties...in the midst of the coming crises...in perilous times..."I will deliver you!" This is God's Word to you today in the financial problems you are facing.

We do not need to be fearful in times of financial need or concerning the great financial crisis that is coming. God has promised, *"They shall not be ashamed in the evil time: and in the days of famine they shall be satisfied" (Psalm 37:19).*

God's Word says we will be able to laugh at famine and destruction (*Job 5:22*).

These promises belong to you! This is God's Covenant of Blessing and Prosperity with you.

There are many Christians today who are not reaping God's promises of blessing and prosperity because they have not kept their covenant with God and have failed to fulfill their vows...the pledges they have made to God and His work.

There are thousands of Christians within the Body of Christ who have attended seminars, conferences or special meetings in their local churches and have made pledges based upon emotion, with every intention of fulfilling them. However, for various reasons they have not fulfilled them. As a result, they have stopped the flow of God's blessings in their lives. God's Word says:

"When you vow a vow or make a pledge to God, do not put off paying it; for God has no pleasure in fools (those who wit-lessly mock Him). Pay what you vow. It is better that you should not vow than that you should vow and not pay. Do not allow your mouth to cause your body to sin, and do not say be-fore the messenger (the priest) that it was an error or mistake.

Why should God be (made) angry at your voice and destroy the work of your hands?" (Ecclesiastes 5:4-6, TAB).

When you fail to pay any pledge you have made to God, how can God bless you and the work of your hands?

God's promises to us are dependent upon our faithfulness and obedience to Him. He has promised that if we are faithful in paying our vows to Him, then we will be able to call upon Him and He will deliver us. He has promised that if we are faithful in giving our tithes and offerings, then He will rebuke the devourer and open the windows of heaven and pour out a blessing you will not have room enough to contain.

As we enter this decade of the nineties, where God has shown us we are going to face this great financial crisis, our position of strength is going to be our faithfulness and obedience in our giving to God. If you have any unpaid pledges, this is the time to take care of them before this crisis hits. Then you will be able to stand on God's Word and believe God to supernaturally supply your needs.

It is time for God's people to stop limiting God!

God has promised a time of restoration where He is going to shake the nations and give the wealth of the nations to His people. However, before this happens, remember the four phases I told you the Body of Christ is going to experience before restoration?

1. Repentance
2. Separation, Consecration
3. Holiness
4. Restitution, Restoration

Before the Body of Christ can take hold of the wealth He has promised to give us in this endtime harvest, we must come to God in repentance.

We need to repent of limiting Him through our unbelief.

We need to repent of our failure to believe and act on His promises.

We need to repent of our disobedience in failing to keep our covenant with Him.

We need to repent for withholding our tithes and offerings and paying our vows to Him.

After God's people begin to fast and pray and repent,

then will the heavens open up and God will pour out the former and latter rains...the Holy Spirit will be poured out upon all flesh (*Joel 2:13-28*). After God's people have humbled themselves and repented, then will come the promised restoration – God will restore all the things Satan has stolen; then will come an abundance, then God's people will be satisfied! (*Joel 2:24-27*).

There are many Christians today who are frustrated and don't understand why they are not reaping God's promises of blessing and prosperity. They are claiming His promises, but they are failing to keep their covenant with God and are not following the principles God has established concerning giving. As a result, they are not reaping God's promises.

We do not have the right and cannot expect to reap God's blessings if we are not faithful in giving to God and walking in obedience to His Word.

The key to taking possession of the prosperity God has promised and already provided for us is giving...giving to God wholeheartedly, in obedience to His Word. We are to give freely and liberally to God, believing, expecting, trusting God to fulfill His promises and keep His covenant with us.

We will reap what we sow! If we withhold from God and give sparingly, we will reap sparingly. Jesus said, *"Give, and it will be given to you. A good measure, pressed down, shaken together and running over, will be poured into your lap. For with the measure you use, it will be measured to you"* (*Luke 6:38, NIV*).

As we are faithful to God's Word and give liberally and generously, we will reap God's abundance. However, when we withhold from God, it leads to poverty and want. *"There are those who (generously) scatter abroad, and yet increase more; there are those who withhold more than is fitting or what is justly due but it tends only to want"* (*Proverbs 11:24, TAB*).

A financial crisis of major proportions is coming to the so-called Church and so-called Christians! We are going to reap what we have sown. We are going to reap a whirlwind of God's judgment, just as Israel did, because of our disobedience in failing to give our tithes and offerings to God.

America has approximately 100 million professing Christians, with an average annual income of $15-20,000 each, which is roughly $2 trillion. When you multiply that amount by ten percent, it is $200 billion annually in tithes for missions, to feed and clothe the poor, to evangelize the world!

Judgment is coming upon the Church. We have been robbing God! Within the Body of Christ there is only a very small percentage of Christians who are faithful in giving their tithes and offerings to God. How can we expect Him to deliver us and meet our needs during this coming financial crisis when we have broken our covenant and withheld our tithes and offerings from Him?

How can we expect God to pour out His blessings upon us and use us to finance this endtime harvest if we have not been faithful with what He has already given us?

It is time for us to repent! If you have been delinquent or unfaithful in giving your tithes and offerings into His storehouse...the work of God around the world...you need to first ask God to forgive you and rededicate and consecrate your finances to Him. Pay all your pledges and begin now to be faithful in giving your tithes and offerings to God. Don't wait until this financial crisis hits and expect God's blessings to be upon you. Do it now!

God wants you to break Satan's hold on your finances and get out of debt now. He wants to pour out His blessings upon you so that not only will your needs be met, but you will be able to help finance this endtime harvest and be used in evangelizing and winning untold thousands of souls around the world to Christ!

We need to rise up in faith to make a new dedication and consecration of ourselves to God of all that we are and possess...including our finances. In this endtime harvest God is raising up a holy remnant of people through whom He is going to fulfill His will upon the earth.

He is calling us to enter into a Covenant of Blessing and Prosperity with Him. This involves more than just routinely giving tithes and offerings into the local church. Remember, the Church is not a building or denomination. It is an organism. It is the work of God around the world.

God is looking for men and women like Joshua and Caleb, *"who followed the Lord fully,"* who were 100 percent consecrated to Him, who have faith to believe and take hold of His promises. He is looking for people who will become His endtime financiers and will dedicate their finances in fulfilling the divine mandate He has given us of evangelizing the world.

There is coming an avalanche of wealth and God's blessings, unlike anything we have ever seen before, to finance the endtime harvest.

Are you ready to receive it?

Are you ready to break the hold Satan has on your finances?

God is going to shake the nations and cause the wealth of the nations to come to His people! It does not belong to the wicked. God has been saving it for us. However, He is not going to release our finances and pour out His blessings and prosperity upon us so that we can heap them upon ourselves or so we can hoard them. One of the reasons many Christians today are not receiving is because they are selfish in their asking. They are only concerned about their own needs instead of fulfilling the work of God around the world. James said: *"Ye ask, and receive not, because ye ask amiss, that ye may consume it upon your lusts"* (James 4:3).

God is raising up a holy remnant of people who are 100 percent consecrated and sold out to Him, through whom He can pour great wealth and blessings to finance the endtime harvest. The wicked, unbelieving generation today is not going to do it. God wants to do it through us.

It does not matter who you are or what your finances are right now. You may be a housewife, nurse, secretary, maid, doctor, lawyer, mechanic, truck driver...it doesn't matter. God will raise you up and pour out His prosperity and blessings upon you in this endtime harvest and people will know that in the midst of great financial crisis God has a people. People will look at you and know that you are a child of the living God!

Isaiah prophesied: *"And their offspring shall be known among the nations, and their descendants among the peo-*

ples. All who see them (in their prosperity) will recognize and acknowledge that they are the people whom the Lord has blessed" (Isaiah 61:9, TAB).

Break Satan's hold on your finances!

Our position of strength, as we enter the decade of the nineties and face this great financial crisis, is in our covenant relationship with God...where we are walking in obedience to Him and His Word...where we are living in continual fellowship with Him...where we are giving, believing, expecting and trusting Him to keep His covenant with us.

I believe that as we enter this decade of spiritual destiny God wants you to get out of debt. How can you help finance the endtime harvest when you cannot pay your bills? In the days to come, God's people need to be out of debt. We need to get rid of the credit cards with their high interest rates that are keeping people in bondage.

I believe that as you rise up in faith to a new level of consecration and dedication to God of yourself...your time...talent...finances...and join in a covenant with God as one of His endtime financiers, you are going to break the hold Satan has on your finances! As God's servant, there are two things I want you to do this month:

1. Take a piece of paper and write down the total amount of money you owe. Then write down how much money you need for the personal needs of yourself and your family. Underneath that, write down how much money you would like to have to give into God's work. Add these figures together and circle the total amount. Put it in your Bible and every time you see it, release your faith and believe God for that amount.

   Don't limit God!

2. As we begin this Decade of Spiritual Destiny, I challenge you to join together with God in His Covenant of Blessing and Prosperity by making a new dedication and consecration of your finances as one of His endtime financiers. Release your faith and believe God is going to break Satan's hold on your finances Get ready to receive an outpouring of God's blessings in your life!

Total Money Owed

1.Cars	–	$ 7,320
2. Credit Cards	–	$ 4,311
3. House	–	$ 22,400
4. Business Expenses	–	$ 2,600
Total	–	$ 36,631
Personal and Family Needs	–	$ 1,750 Per Month
I want to give to God	–	$ 400 per month

It is time for you to walk in the knowledge that you are living in the greatest hour of spiritual destiny the Church has ever known.

Take your position as part of the holy remnant God is raising up!

Therefore be ye also ready; for in such an hour as ye think not the son of man cometh" (Matthew 24:44).

Chapter 6

Crisis 5: A Satanic Confrontation Of Gigantic Proportions

We are entering into the greatest time of spiritual destiny the Church has ever known! We are headed for a final showdown. Simultaneously, as the power of the Holy Spirit is being poured out upon the Body of Christ, Satan will be intensifying his attacks and with great fury will be pouring out his wrath through his demon principalities.

These two spiritual forces...God's power and the power of Satan...are both intensifying and coming to a great climax where God is going to totally crush Satan and his kingdom and remove every trace of evil from this earth.

Satan is a liar and a counterfeit!

Just as God is building His Army, Satan is building his army.

Just as God is intensifying His work today and we are going to see an endtime outpouring of His Spirit through signs and wonders, Satan is also intensifying his work and we will see a flood of **lying** signs and wonders.

Just as God's people are proclaiming the true Gospel of Jesus Christ around the world, Satan is promoting a false message...doctrines of demons...through his followers.

Satan and his demonic forces are organized and prepared to make a final assault! He has strategically placed men and women in every phase of society to influence and propagate his demonic doctrines.

There are no "schisms" in Satan's army! Satan and his legions of demons and evil principalities are all united together for one purpose...to deceive every person upon the face of the earth and lead the world in a final rebellion against God.

Paul said, *"We wrestle not against flesh and blood, but*

against principalities, against powers, against the rulers of the darkness of this world, against spiritual wickedness in high places" (Ephesians 6:12).
These demons...evil principalities, rulers of darkness of this world, spiritual wickedness in high places...give their sole allegiance to Satan. They carry out his orders explicitly and without question.
Don't fool yourself! We are not fighting an enemy that is unorganized, undisciplined, disjointed or haphazard in fulfilling Satan's plan and purposes. Satan's army of demons is highly organized into various ranks, with specific purposes to fulfill, and are functioning together in unity under Satan as their supreme head.
Satan is the *"prince of the power of the air" (Ephesians 2:2).* These powers, principalities, rulers of darkness, and spiritual wickedness in high places – hover over our cities and fill the atmosphere with their evil influence. They have been dispatched and assigned to work in specific cities, governments, schools and administrations.
As these two spiritual forces...God's power and the power of Satan...continue to grow and intensify, we are going to face the greatest assault from Satan and his demon principalities that man has ever known or experienced!
The fifth major crisis God has shown me is coming in the nineties is one of satanic confrontation...of intensified spiritual warfare.
The Body of Christ will face satanic confrontation greater than at any other time in history. It will be a time of intensified spiritual warfare where demons will manifest themselves and will be in direct confrontation with God's people.
In a vision, God showed John an endtime war when Satan and his angels would be cast down to the earth, where he would make war against God's people.
"And the dragon (Satan) was wroth with the woman, and went to make war with the remnant of her seed, which keep the commandments of God, and have the testimony of Jesus Christ" (Revelation 12:17).
Today Satan, knowing that he only has a short time, is pouring out his fury upon the Body of Christ. For years I

have been warning that Satan has declared war on the Church and have been teaching how to declare war on the devil's war!

During this coming crisis of satanic confrontation, there will be a strong wave of deception that will sweep across the world so strongly that millions will be deceived, including many so-called Christians. Unless Christians have a strong foundation that is based upon the infallible, impregnable Word of God, they will be deceived and fall away from the faith.

Paul told Timothy: *"Now the Spirit speaketh expressly, that in the latter times some shall depart from the faith, giving heed to seducing spirits, and **doctrines of devils**"* (*I Timothy 4:1*).

He warned: *"For the time will come when they will not endure sound doctrine: but after their own lusts shall they heap to themselves teachers, having itching ears, **And they shall turn away their ears from the truth, and shall be turned unto fables**"* (*II Timothy 4:3-4*).

Paul told Timothy, *"But evil men and seducers shall wax worse and worse, deceiving, and being deceived"* (*II Timothy 3:13*).

John warned the believers, *"For many deceivers are entered into the world, who confess not that Jesus Christ is come in the flesh. This is a deceiver and an antichrist"* (*II John 2:7*).

The Spirit of God is very clear and specific. We are going to face such an onslaught of lying, seducing, deceiving spirits, there will be many professing Christians who are going to "depart" from the faith. Paul said there will be those who will turn away their ears from hearing the truth. They are going to be seduced and deceived into accepting the lies and false doctrines of devils.

This wave of satanic deception will be so strong that if it were possible, even the **elect**...the endtime remnant would be deceived. Jesus warned that this would be one of the signs of His coming. He said: *"False Christs (Messiahs) and false prophets will arise and show signs and (work) miracles to deceive and lead astray, if possible, even the elect, those God has chosen out for Himself. But look to yourselves and* *be on your guard*; *I have told you everything beforehand"* (*Mark 13:22-23, TAB*).

Jesus said, "Be on your guard." He has revealed to us we are going to face this demonic assault of lying, deceptive, seducing spirits that will be working through false christs and false prophets so that we will be prepared. If we fail to guard our hearts and minds against these demon spirits, we are setting ourselves up for defeat!

Do not think for one moment that you are so spiritually strong you are beyond the point of ever being deceived. No one is going to be exempt from this onslaught of the enemy. Satan and his demon principalities are trying to deceive the whole world and will be focusing their attacks especially upon God's "elect"...the choice servants of God.

Satan Has Released An Army Of Demon Spirits!

The Spirit of God revealed to John in a vision how, in the last days, demon spirits would be released upon the earth which would go forth to deceive the world. John said: *"And I saw three unclean spirits like frogs come out of the mouth of the dragon, and out of the mouth of the beast, and out of the mouth of the false prophet" (Revelation 16:13).*

These three spirits that John saw represent lying, deceiving, seducing demon spirits that are going to be released by Satan, the Antichrist and the false prophet. In *verse 14*, John further explains what these spirits are and their purpose. He said: *"For they are the spirits of devils, working miracles, which go forth unto the kings of the earth and of the whole world, to gather them to the battle of that great day of God Almighty" (Revelation 16:14).*

Today, Satan has commissioned and sent forth an army of lying, deceiving, seducing spirits into this world who are now working through men and women, teaching "doctrines of demons," seducing and leading men and women away from the truth and away from God. By the means of counterfeit, lying signs and wonders, these spirits will deceive many and cause them to believe Satan's lies.

This wave of satanic deception will be so strong that the whole world will be deceived into worshipping Satan and the Antichrist.

In the decade of the nineties, Satan and his principalities will intensify their activities...perverting the truth...opposing the work of God...persecuting the saints...lying...propagating heresies and false doctrines...deceiving and turning men's hearts against God, until one day all those upon the face of the earth who are not born again will worship Satan and the Antichrist.

"And they worshiped the dragon (Satan) which gave power unto the beast: (Antichrist) and they worshiped the beast saying, Who is like unto the beast? who is able to make war with him?...And all that dwell upon the earth shall worship him, whose names are not written in the book of life of the Lamb slain from the foundation of the world" *(Revelation 13:4,8).*

It is later than you think! We are not far away from seeing these prophecies fulfilled upon the earth! Most Christians think of the coming of the Antichrist as being some time in the far-distant future. It isn't!

The **spirit** of antichrist is here now upon this earth! There is not one sphere of influence on this earth that it has not infiltrated.

The apostle John told the believers, *"...every spirit that confesseth not that Jesus Christ is come in the flesh is not of God: **and this is that spirit of antichrist** whereof ye have heard that it should come; and even now already is it in the world"* *(I John 4:3).*

In this verse John was not referring directly to the Antichrist himself, but to the **spirit** of antichrist that was already working upon the earth at that time! The word "antichrist" in Greek is "antichristos," which means "against Christ" or "instead of Christ." The spirit of antichrist denies the very existence of the one true God.

John said, *"Children, it is the last hour; and just as you heard that antichrist is coming, even now many antichrists have arisen; from this we know that it is the last hour"* *(I John 2:18, NAS).* Just as there were antichrists, deceivers, seducers, false teachers at that time...people who denied that Jesus was the Messiah, the Son of God, there are many antichrists today who recognize Jesus as a prophet and a good man but do not acknowledge him as the Son of God.

John said, *"Who is a liar but he that denieth that Jesus is the Christ? He is antichrist, that denieth the Father and the Son"* *(I John 2:22)*.

For thousands of years the spirit of antichrist has been working upon the earth. There have been many antichrists, false christs, seducers and deceivers. There are many antichrists **now** upon the earth.

The spirit of antichrist is actively working today to oppose Christ and Christianity, to establish a godless society that denies the existence of God, to elevate man as a god unto himself, to deceive men and women into believing heresies and false doctrines. The spirit of antichrist opposes the truth and substitutes lies. We can see the influence of this antichrist spirit all around us!

The spirit of antichrist has been working and will continue to work in the decade of the nineties preparing the way for the coming Antichrist...the beast...the man described in Revelation 13:4-8, who will be empowered by Satan to establish his kingdom upon the earth for a short period of time. This coming Antichrist will oppose God, exalt himself above God and set himself up as God (II Thessalonians 2:4; Daniel 11:36).

He will come into power peaceably: *"And in his estate shall stand up a vile person, to whom they shall not give the honor of the kingdom:* **but he shall come in peaceably** *and obtain the kingdom by flatteries"* *(Daniel 11:21)*.

And, through lying signs and wonders, he will deceive the world: *"Even him, whose coming is after the working of Satan with all power and signs and lying wonders, And with all deceivableness of unrighteousness in them that perish; because they received not the love of the truth, that they might be saved"* *(II Thessalonians 2:9-10)*.

Paul told the Thessalonians that this coming Antichrist would be revealed before Christ's coming.

He said: *"Now we beseech you, brethren,* **by the coming of our Lord Jesus Christ, and by our gathering together unto him**, *That ye be not soon shaken in mind, or be troubled, neither by spirit, nor by word, nor by letter as from us, as that the day of Christ is at hand.* **Let no man deceive you by any means: for that day shall not come,** *except there come a falling away first, and that man of sin be revealed, the son of perdition; Who opposeth and exalteth himself above all that is called God, or that is worshiped; so that he as God sitteth in the temple of God, showing himself that he is God" (II Thessalonians 2:1-4).*

In these verses Paul states clearly and specifically that the day of the Lord, when Christ will return to earth to gather His saints unto Himself and pour out the wrath of God upon the wicked, will not come until the Antichrist is revealed.

Every day we draw one step closer to this time when the coming Antichrist will set up his kingdom upon the earth!

Every day we are one day nearer that great day when Christ is going to burst through the clouds and descend from heaven with a shout, with the voice of the archangel. The trumpet of God is going to blast through the air and we are going to be caught up to meet Him in the air! (I Thessalonians 4:16).

In The Nineties We Will See A Continued Increase In Occultic And Demonic Activities

It is time for us to shake ourselves out of the spiritual stupor we have been in. It is time for us to recognize the lateness of the hour in which we live!

While the Church has become distracted, disjointed, fragmented...while we have been warring among ourselves... Satan and his army of demon principalities have been feverishly working night and day following a well-organized plan to bring the whole world into rebellion against God.

While the Church, as a whole, has failed to recognize the reality of Satan's power and his work upon the earth, Satan and his army have been busy fulfilling his diabolical plan.

While Christian leaders, pastors, ministers of the Gospel and believers have been afraid to expose Satan and the reality of demon spirits for fear of being accused of going off the deep end or seeing a demon "behind every bush," Satan and his demons have been busy multiplying and building his kingdom...preparing the way for the coming Antichrist.

While Christians have been afraid or have failed to take their position of power and authority over Satan and his demons, Satan has been having a heyday wreaking havoc in their lives...attacking their bodies, their families, their finances and opposing the work of God around the world.

In the past ten-fifteen years, there has been a revival of Satanism and the occult.

Satan and demon worship is not a new "religion." As the Israelites became intermingled with the heathen nations, they were polluted and began to worship idol gods. There were even some who sacrificed their children to devils.

"And they served their idols: which were a snare unto them. Yea, they sacrificed their sons and their daughters unto devils, And shed innocent blood, even the blood of their sons and of their daughters, whom they sacrificed unto the idols of Canaan: and the land was polluted with blood" (Psalm 106:36-38).

The apostle Paul warned Christians in the early Church not to eat or drink things which the Gentiles sacrificed to devils. He said: *"But I say, that the things which the Gentiles sacrifice, they sacrifice to devils, and not to God: and I would not that ye should not have fellowship with devils. Ye cannot drink the cup of the Lord, and the cup of devils: ye cannot be partakers of the Lord's table, and of the table of devils" (I Corinthians 10:20-21).*

Throughout the ages, Satan has always had a counterfeit religion based upon idol gods, demon worship, magic, witchcraft and the occult. During the decade of the seventies, as the Church was experiencing a revival...a wave of the Holy Spirit in the "Charismatic" movement, there was also a revival of the occult.

In The Decade Of The Nineties A Revival Of The Occult Will Continue!

In the decade of the nineties...

We will see a tremendous growth in Satanism and the occult. Its influence will continue to spread into all phases of our society and will be recognized as an acceptable form of religion.

Satanic rituals involving animal and human sacrifices will continue to increase.

Satanic crimes related to Satan worship will increase.

Hospital first to offer treatment for teens caught in satanic web

Associated Press

CHICAGO — At his parents' home, Mike painted his room black, decorated it with black candles and an altar, and put up obituaries and satanic symbols on the walls.

He began driving recklessly, drinking heavily, experimenting with researching satanic beliefs for three years and was contracted to set up Hartgrove's center.

"The factors that seem to be adding to a growth of the occult don't. seem to be going away — a breakdown in family, an abandonment of traditional values, resistance toward traditional religious beliefs and an

In Chicago, a special hospital wing was recently opened to help young people escape from Satanism.

More and more witches and their covens will continue to come out of the closet...out of hiding, and will actively promote witchcraft and openly recruit others.

There will be a growing number of occult-related movies and videos.

In 1972, *Time* magazine featured a cover story on the growth of Satan worship and the occult. On the cover of the magazine was a man in a dark hood with a satanic pentagram and a goat's head painted on it. The large bold headlines read **"The Occult Revival"**..."**Satan Returns.**" This article reported on the "wave of fascination with the occult" which was sweeping through the United States at that time.

The article reported on the increased popularity of occult bookshops and centers, teaching workshops on tarot card readings, palmistry, reincarnation and astral projections. It pointed out the fact that major publishers had issued dozens of hardcover books on the occult and parapsychology that past year. Since the introduction of the occult movie "Rosemary's Baby" in 1968, the article stated there had been a series of movies based on the occult. The au-

103

thor stated, "But the interest goes beyond books and movies: a growing number of colleges across the United States are offering courses on aspects of the occult."

In the early seventies, the Church and School of Wicca, one of the most active witchcraft movements in America, opened and the school has been operating as a tax-exempt institution since 1972. Today it is estimated that there are fifty to one hundred thousand members of Wicca who actively practice witchcraft in the United States.

In the mid-seventies, there were reports about finding sheep, cattle and horses who had been slaughtered and their blood drained.

This renewed interest in the occult which began in the seventies was not just a coincidence. It did not just happen. It was just the beginning of a revival of Satanism and the occult.

In 1988, on a national talk show, several women gave their testimonies that they were kept by satanic cults to breed babies to sacrifice to Satan.

In the eighties, the number of occult-related and horror movies filled with violence and satanic ritualized murders grew in number and popularity. "Ghostbusters" featured a scene where a woman was levitated and a demon spoke through her. The most successful of these movies was a series, "Nightmare On Elm Street," featuring a child molester, Freddy Krueger, who murdered innocent children. The original version earned $24 million and the first three installments brought in $103 million.

In the decade of the eighties, Satanism and the occult continued to grow. In 1980, *Newsweek* magazine reported accounts of mutilated livestock in 27 states which were related to Satanism.

The number of crimes related to Satan worship also increased during the decade of the eighties. Reports of ritual abuse of children continue to grow. In 1985, after treating young patients, Dr. Gregory Simpson, a Los Angeles pediatrician, began a study on the ritual abuse of children. He stated, "The conclusion I reached is that satanic abuse of small children does exist, and it is something that needs to be dealt with in the medical community." Cult watchers and police agree that a large number of missing children today are victims of human sacrifice cults.

Satan worship-related crimes, such as that of Sean Sellers, age 16, convicted in 1986 of three murders, including his parents, are growing in number. The night before Sean picked up a revolver, walked into his parents' room and cold-bloodedly shot both of his parents in the head, laughing as he watched the blood pour out of his mother's head, he went through his satanic rituals and called up spirits and asked them to enter his body.

Another example of these satanic crimes is the case in 1987 where three boys, after sacrificing a cat to Satan, turned on another boy, chanting "Sacrifice for Satan." They chased him down, beat him to death with baseball bats and threw his body into a cistern with the dead cat.

These types of ritualistic Satan-related crimes are at an all-time high. In a 1980 *Newsweek* article, "Networking to Beat the Devil," Chicago police detective, Robert Simandl, feels that satanic crime will be the crime of the nineties. A network of over 1,000 officers and counselors have formed to share information on occult-related crimes. Detective Simandl has conducted more than 200 seminars for law enforcement professionals on how to detect occult involvement in crimes.

One of Satan's major targets in this revival of Satanism and the occult is our young people. According to the president of National Information Network, 30 to 40 percent of high school students are involved in some form of the occult. They are being enticed and lured into Satanism through drugs, occultic games, movies and demon-inspired hard rock and black metal music featuring songs filled with blasphemy, demons and violence.

On a popular radio show in San Diego, "Talk Back With Bob Larson," a young Satan-worshiper admitted that he was introduced to Satanism by listening to the black metal band "Slayer." He said, "**When I was young, Slayer brought Satanism into my life. It is because of their music that I worship the devil. Their lyrics introduced me to Lord**

Increased experimentation in psychic phenomena will take place in the Decade of Destiny!

Satan. They made me what I am. The words of their songs are the most important thing to me."[1]

Although Satan's major seduction and deception during this revival of the occult has been aimed at introducing young people into the occult and Satan worship, our society has been saturated with occultic influences which open the door and lead to further involvement with the occult. Along with the strong growth of this occultic influence in the past decade, has come a more widespread acceptance of the occult-related activities such as palmistry, astrology, channeling, visualization, yoga, meditation, self-hypnosis, astro projection, and other forms of psychic phenomena.

Nancy Reagan's involvement with astrology made national headlines and actress Shirley MacLaine starred in a film and wrote a book about her experiences in "channeling" a demon spirit. Millions of people today follow their astrological horoscopes religiously.According to Congressman Charlie Ross, about one-fourth of the members of Congress at any given time are actively interested in psy-

1. Reprinted by permission from Bob Larson's book, *Seduction of America's Youth*

chic phenomena, including psychic healing, prophecy, remote viewing or physical manifestations of psychic power.

This increased interest and growth of Satanism and the occult is not just a passing fad. It is all part of Satan's diabolical plan to "set the stage" for the coming Antichrist. The Church cannot continue to close its eyes at what is happening!

Beyond this revival of the occult is an even more subtle and deceptive strategy involving the establishment of a one-world religion and the initiation of a "New Age" and a "New Age Messiah" through the rapidly growing New Age Movement.

Satan's Counterfeit Religion Is Here!

While the Church has been sleeping...denying or ignoring the reality of a devil and his demons...Satan and his army have been setting the stage for the coming of the Antichrist!

Tens of millions of New Age believers are eagerly anticipating and looking for the soon appearing of a New Age "Christ" or "Messiah" upon the earth. They believe that the world is on the threshold of a radical spiritual transformation...a global crisis...that will usher in the "Age of Aquarius" or the "New Age."

New Age believers believe that after this global crisis, when the world is in chaos, its "Messiah" or "Great World Teacher" will come bringing peace, unity and prosperity and lead man into a glorious New Age with a one-world government and a one-world religion. They believe this New Age "Christ" will possess unparalleled wisdom, marvelous psychic abilities and the powers of the universe will be at his command.

The establishment of this new kingdom on earth under this New Age "Christ" is believed to be on the near horizon. Some believe the "Messiah" will make his appearance in the year 2000, while others believe it may occur at any time.

John Randolph Price, head of two major New Age groups – The Quartus Foundation For Spiritual Research and The Planetary Commission For Global Healing – has stated concerning the coming of the New Age "Christ": "The gathering is taking place. (New Age believers) in all religions are uniting again – this time in a New Commission to reveal the Light of the World...and begin the Aquarian Age of Spirituality on Planet Earth."[2]

On December 31, 1986, millions of New Age followers worldwide gathered in stadiums, convention halls, meeting rooms and in churches to bring in this New Age. This "International Meditation Day" was sponsored by hundreds of New Age organizations in sixty nations of the world. As they gathered throughout the world to "meditate," thousands of them called for the New Age "Christ" to come forth.

On January 12, 1987, the following copy, prepared by the Tara Center, appeared in a full-page ad in *USA TODAY:*

"Drugs...AIDS...poverty...rampant crime...mass starvation...nuclear threat...terrorism...Is there a solution? In answer to our urgent need...the Christ is in the world. A great World Teacher for people of every religion and no religion, a practical man with solutions to our problems. He loves all humanity...Christ is here, my friends. Your brother walks among you."

Simultaneously, as God's people are looking for the second coming of Jesus Christ, Satan is disguising and preparing a counterfeit...a counterfeit religion and a counterfeit "Christ" through whom he can work to deceive the world into worshipping him.

The New Age Movement with its coming New Age "Christ" is not a small, insignificant, isolated group like those false "Christ" cults we have seen spring up in the past and soon disappear from sight. Within the past ten years, it has experienced a phenomenal growth and has become a worldwide network of believers, estimated to be about onehalf billion strong, from all walks of life, including teachers, office workers, famous scientists, celebrities, government officials. There are those who are leaders in medicine, education, law and psychology. There are New Age believers in large corporations, universities, public schools and on the White House staff.

One of the reasons for its rapid growth is the fact that it is a religion that incorporates many people from all religions, such as Buddhists, Shintoists, Satanists, humanists,

2. *Reprinted by permission from Texe Marrs' book, "Dark Secrets of the New Age."*

witches, witch doctors, Hindus and all other types of religions, **excluding only Christianity and those who believe in Jesus Christ and a personal God.**

Their major goal as they await their coming "Messiah" is to work through a large number of separate organizations to subvert and destroy biblical Christianity and replace it with a one-world religion based upon scientific laws and Eastern mysticisms. Their objectives are to undermine the credibility of the Bible, discredit Jesus Christ and weaken Christian churches.

This Satan-inspired religion teaches:

There is no sin and evil.

A personal God does not exist.

Jesus was not the Son of God.

His sacrifice on the cross was meaningless.

Man does not need a savior.

Man is himself an evolving god.

Since they believe there is no evil or sin, and don't believe in Satan as an evil force, they do not believe in a literal burning hell. New Age teachers recognize Lucifer as the "light bringer" and praise him as the "bright and morning star." One of the leading New Age teachers, David Spangler, teaches that it is Lucifer who initiates and leads converts into the New Age religion. He explains: "Lucifer comes to give us the final...luciferic initiation...that many people in the days ahead will be facing, for it is an invitation into the New Age."[3] During their meditations, many New Age believers center their minds on the phrases, "Come, Lucifer" or "Come, 666."

Paul told Timothy in the time of great apostasy men would be deceived by *"seducing spirits and doctrines of devils" (I Timothy 4:1).* This New Age doctrine is being preached throughout the world by what the New Agers are calling "spirit guides," "masters," "wise ones," "light bearers," "inner guides," who are actually lying demon spirits which have taken possession of individuals and are spewing forth their lies.

Thousands are flocking to seminars, paying as much as $400 per seminar, to hear these demon spirits. The New Age teaches that these demon spirits or "wise ones" are sent to guide mankind to the **truth**. In actuality, they are lying, seducing, deceiving spirits who have been released by Satan to deceive people into believing and accepting his lies and his counterfeit religion. This is the spirit of antichrist working!

New Age believers call this communication with demon spirits "channeling." They are taught to make contact with these demons through meditation. Most New Age teachers encourage new converts to empty their minds and let a "Presence" come in which will be their "inner guide." Demons masquerading as saints such as Jonah, Isaiah, Paul, John, and even a false Jesus, have come to New Age believers while they were meditating.

These demons are declaring a personal God does not exist, man is evolving into gods and that Jesus was not the Son of God but is the Christ consciousness within us. Millions of New Age believers are regularly communicating with these demons.

The World Is Ready To Accept A One-World Religion!

The stage is now being set for Satan's counterfeit religion! The New Age Movement has become a monstrous network of many different organizations spreading its blasphemous lies throughout the world. The major lies being propagated and accepted by millions of people deny Jesus' sacrifice on the cross, deny His resurrection and deny the real second coming of Jesus. Emmett Fox, formerly a prominent liberal Christian minister, who is now a popular New Age teacher, has written:

"The Christ is not Jesus. The Christ is the active presence of God – in living men and women...In the history of all races the Cosmic Christ had incarnated in man – Buddha, Moses, Elijah and in many other leaders...However, in this New Age, the Cosmic Christ will come into millions of men and women who are ready to receive it. This will be the second coming of Christ for them."[4]

Satan's master plan of establishing his counterfeit religion is deception. The message the New Age is using to deceive

3. & 4. *Reprinted by permission from Texe Marrs' book,* Dark Secrets of the New Age.

millions is world peace, unity and prosperity. In a time of great political and economic upheaval, with the foreboding threat of a nuclear war looming on the horizon, and nations on the brink of economic crises, the nations of the world are looking for peace and are ready to accept the one-world view with a one-world government merged with a one-world religion being propagated by the New Age Movement.

We are living in the hour Paul referred to when men would turn their ears away from the truth (*II Thessalonians 2:12*)

As the New Age Movement continues to spread its doctrine, there are going to be many church organizations and Christians who are going to compromise and turn away from the truth for the sake of world unity and peace. Christians who refuse to compromise with the Eastern religions and take a firm stand that Jesus is the Son of God and that He is the only way of salvation are going to be looked upon as "separatists" who are a threat to achieving world peace and will be ostracized and persecuted. The apostate church will merge together with the New Age Movement and Eastern religions.

The objective of the New Age Movement is to replace Christianity with the New Age world religion. New Age converts are encouraged to stay in their churches and to transform them from **within**. The New Age is now infiltrating churches by planting "Cosmic Christians"...people who pretend to be Christians but who are sent by Satan to bring confusion and to introduce New Age doctrine.

The New Age Movement has already succeeded in making major inroads into mainline Christian denominations, evangelical seminaries, and Bible book stores. Satan has deceived pastors and Christian leaders into accepting and preaching messages incorporating principles that are part of the New Age doctrine. There are many so-called "Christian" authors who are writing books promoting New Age teachings and their books are being sold in Christian bookstores.

There are Christians today who have become involved in holistic health and nutrition, biofeedback, astrological horoscopes, yoga, hypnosis, and martial arts, which are all "offshoots" of the New Age and are based upon some of the same principles that are being taught by the New Age.

Holistic health and nutrition involves developing the mind, emotions, and the physical aspects of the body and unifying the whole body. The deception here is in the fact that the individual is not looking to Christ for healing but the emphasis is on self...on the individual's ability to control his own health.

Biofeedback is a machine that gives an individual feedback on his body's systems, so that he can control them. Here again, the emphasis is on man's ability to control his own health and replaces his dependence upon God.

Yoga and the martial arts such as karate and kung-fu, are not just physical conditioning exercises. These exercises are based upon Eastern mysticism and requires an individual to draw upon a form of energy beyond himself. When you become involved in these, you are actually bringing into your system energy from a satanic source.

Jesus warned that deception in the last days would be so great that, if possible, even the elect would be deceived: *"For false Christs and false prophets shall rise, and shall show signs and wonders, to seduce, if it were possible, even the elect" (Mark 13:22).*

We are living in a day when a Christian cannot be sure he is in a Christ-centered, Spirit-filled congregation just because he is a member of a particular denomination that claims to be Christian. Neither can a Christian accept everything being taught or preached from the pulpit as truth.

God's people must begin to exercise spiritual discernment. The apostle John said, *"Beloved, do not believe every spirit, but test the spirits to see whether they are from God; because many false prophets have gone out into the world" (I John 4:1, NAS).* You cannot afford to accept every new doctrine that comes along.

John told the believers, *"...every spirit that confesseth not that Jesus Christ is come in the flesh is not of God: and this is that spirit of antichrist" (I John 4:3).*

Any doctrine that draws you away from Christ and causes you to put self on the throne of your life is propagated by the spirit of antichrist and you must reject it!

Any doctrine you hear that turns your heart away from Christ and causes you to seek after the world and its material possessions is being propagated by the spirit of antichrist...reject it!

Any doctrine that causes you to seek after power so that you can try to manipulate God in acquiring things for self is being propagated by the spirit of antichrist...don't accept it!

The New Age Movement teaches a personal God does not exist, that man is a god, and to focus on the "Christ consciousness" within himself. Any doctrine that teaches you to focus upon self instead of Jesus Christ...that teaches you to follow your own will instead of continually dying to self and following God's will...that causes you to put self first...is part of the lies being propagated by the New Age Movement and you must reject it!

In the coming decade of the nineties, as occultic activities continue to increase and multiplied thousands of New Age believers are added and begin to communicate regularly with demon spirits, Christians are going to face direct confrontation with demon spirits.

Simultaneously, as the power of the Holy Spirit is being poured out upon the true Body of Christ and Satan's power intensifies through his demon spirits, there is going to be an all-out spiritual war! There will be manifestations where demon spirits will physically and mentally attack Christians. During this last year, our I Care prayer ministers have already reported a significant increase in phone calls from various parts of the country from Christians who have experienced demonic manifestations in their homes.

In the decade of the nineties, these demonic manifestations and direct confrontations with demons will increase. As they do, there is going to be a wave of the Holy Spirit in a manifestation of signs, wonders, and miracles that will give the Body of Christ the ability to have direct confrontation with Satan and his demons. God's people will not shrink back and be afraid, but will stand up to the power of the enemy.

In the decade of the nineties, we will see a manifestation of Satan's counterfeit lying signs and wonders. Simultaneously, as there is a manifestation of God's power working signs and wonders through the Body of Christ, Satan will be manifesting lying signs and wonders to deceive people into accepting the lies of the New Age religion and the Antichrist would be *"after the working of Satan with all power and signs and lying wonders"* (II Thessalonians 2:9).

The apostle John said it would be through the means of miracles which the false prophet would be able to do that the world would be deceived into worshipping the Antichrist. *"And he doeth great wonders, so that he maketh fire come down from heaven on the earth in the sight of men, And deceiveth them that dwell on the earth **by the means of those miracles** which he had power to do in the sight of the beast (antichrist)"* (Revelation 13:13-14).

As God's miracle power is manifested in divine healing, there will be manifestations of healing through psychic powers as people draw upon the power of Satan. There will be counterfeit manifestations of the Holy Spirit...counterfeit prophecies through demon spirits...counterfeit revelations and counterfeit tongues.

It is time for the Church of Jesus Christ to prepare for this confrontation that is coming! Regardless of whether you believe Christ is coming before, during, or after the time referred to as the tribulation period, what are you doing to warn others of what is coming upon the earth?

What are you doing to prepare yourself?

Satan has set the stage for the coming Antichrist. All the pieces are beginning to fall into place. The nations of the world are in a political and economic upheaval and are desperately seeking solutions. After centuries of repression and denial of the existence of God in many Communist-dominated countries, physical and political barriers have been broken down, opening doors for a short time for religious freedom. The people are looking for something to fill the vacuum in their lives.

We are living in a crisis of change!

The radical changes we are seeing in policies in Russia are happening because of the great economic and sociological problems that have grown to drastic proportions. Gorbachev, a strong adherent to the New Age philosophy, wrote a book in 1987 called "Perestroika...New Thinking For Our Country and the World," which became a national

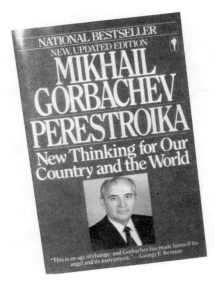

On the cover of Mikhail Gorbachev's book, Perestroika, is the following statement: "This is an age of change; and Gorbachev has made himself its angel and its instrument."

George F. Kennan

best-seller in the United States. This book is actually promoting New Age thinking for the world.

In this book, Gorbachev presents the need for "Perestroika"...restructuring...involving radical changes in every aspect of life in Russia, and presents it as a model for a global restructuring which would unite all the nations together and bring world peace and prosperity.

Gorbachev has stated, "We can and we must rally mankind and facilitate the forming of a global consciousness." The "perestroika" that is taking place in Russia is being influenced by New Age philosophies and is a major step in the world today toward a one-world government under a one-world religion...Satan's counterfeit religion.

The world is desperately looking for global peace and many are willing to compromise anything to achieve it. Daniel prophesied concerning the coming Antichrist *"...but he shall come in peaceably, and obtain the kingdom by flatteries"* (Daniel 11:21). *"...and by peace shall destroy many"* (Daniel 8:25).

Paul told the Thessalonians, *"For when they shall say Peace and safety; then sudden destruction cometh upon* them, *as travail upon a woman with child*; *and they shall not escape" (I Thessalonians 5:3).* We are living in the time of birth pangs as a woman in labor. Labor has started...the fulfillment of endtime prophecies has begun and is going to accelerate until all have been fulfilled!

Satan and his army are ready to establish his counterfeit religion. Millions of New Age believers are anxiously looking for their coming "Messiah" to usher in the New Age of world peace, unity and prosperity. There are millions communicating regularly with demon spirits and spreading their counterfeit gospel.

What are you doing?

Do you really believe Jesus is coming soon? Are you excited about and praying for His coming? Are you ready to stand before Him in His Presence?

I have shared with you the five major crises God has shown me are coming in the nineties:

Crisis 1 – Crisis of Change
Crisis 2 – Crisis of the Family
Crisis 3 – Crisis of the Church
Crisis 4 – Worldwide Financial Crises
Crisis 5 – Crisis of Satanic Confrontation

How are you going to prepare for these crises? God is not warning you to scare you, but to prepare you! Jesus said, when you see all these things begin to take place, to rejoice...lift up your head, your redemption draweth nigh (*Luke 21:28*).

Before I reveal to you the Five Major Waves of the Holy Spirit in the next decade, I would be negligent in my duty as a prophet of God if I did not guide you in how you can be prepared for the oncoming crises...no matter what your current circumstances may be!

In the next chapter, I will reveal to you God's endtime plan, His strategy for preparing you and His Church for the soon coming crises.

Chapter 7

God's Endtime Strategy For The Church

Knowing we are God's people of destiny...knowing we are living in the final count-down...knowing that we have **already** entered into a time of crisis...

We must shake ourselves out of our spiritual sleep and apathy, and rise up in these closing hours of time with a new sense of purpose, a new sense of urgency and a new spiritual determination and consecration to fulfill all that God has planned to do through us.

I have shared with you the Five Major Crises God has shown me are coming in the nineties. What I have shared with you concerning these crises is only the small tip of the iceberg. There is much, much more that God is going to reveal to us in the days to come. As Jesus was preparing His disciples for the crises they were going to face, He told them, *"I have yet many things to say unto you, but ye cannot bear them now" (John 16:12).* Jesus knew they were not spiritually mature or ready at that point to understand everything He had to tell them.

There is more revelation that God wants to give us concerning His plan for us in these endtimes, but He knows the level of our spiritual maturity and how much we can handle. When He gives us revelation, it is so that we will not only accept it but also act on it. As we are faithful to act upon the revelation He gives us, He will give us more.

There are some of you who have read about the crises that are coming and you feel overwhelmed. You don't know how you are going to be able to face what is coming. Before we go any further in this revelation and look at the Five Major Waves of the Holy Spirit that are coming, there is a powerful spiritual strategy God has revealed to

117

me that we must begin using now so that we will be strong and victorious in the days to come. This is God's endtime strategy for the Church!

Strategy 1: God Is Saying To The Body Of Christ: Set A Watch In Prayer!

This is God's message to the Church today as we prepare for His coming. He is commanding us to set a watch in prayer.

In the armed forces, there are soldiers who are assigned special duty as guards to stand watch outside the barracks or command post. The watch is set for around the clock... twenty-four hours a day. Under no circumstances is the soldier to leave his post. The duties of this watchman are:

1. To guard and protect.

2. To be constantly on the alert, watching for any sign of the enemy.

3. To "challenge" everyone, including superior officers, who would try to enter the premises.

4. To warn of danger.

5. To confront and stop the enemy from entering.

God has revealed to us what is coming upon the earth; He has revealed the lateness of the hour; and He is now directing the Body of Christ to set a watch in prayer! It is not something optional He is asking us to do. He requires it of us. And, those who fail to hear and obey what the Spirit of God is saying to His Church today will not be able to stand. They will be taken off guard. They will reap heartache and defeat.

Turn in your Bible to the book of *Mark, chapter thirteen,* and read *verses 28-37*. After revealing the signs of His coming to His disciples...false Christs, wars, earthquakes, famines, persecution, the Gospel being preached to all nations, counterfeit lying signs and wonders, deception, signs in the heavens...Jesus gave a direct command. He said to watch and pray!

First He drew their attention to the fact that these signs He had told them about would be an indicator that His coming was near. There are Christians today who are so concerned with the signs of Jesus' coming...the wars, earthquakes, famines...that they have lost sight of the fact that these signs are God's signal to His endtime remnant that Jesus' coming is at the door and they must prepare themselves.

Our major focus must not be upon these signs. The signs and the crises are inevitable. But in the midst of all these things we must keep our hearts and minds fixed upon the fact that Jesus' coming is at hand. We must be doing everything possible to prepare ourselves for that great day.

Jesus said that just as certainly as we are able to determine that summer is near by the signs of the budding of the trees and the new growth of green leaves, we are able to know that Jesus' coming is imminent when we see these signs come to pass.

Jesus said, *"Surely, I say to you, this generation (the whole multitude of people living at that one time) positively will not perish or pass away before all these things take place" (Mark 13:30, TAB).*

There is a fixed time in God's timetable when He has planned for Christ's return. It is an unalterable fact. Once the prophesied endtime events begin, they will happen rapidly in succession. Nothing will prevent it.

Jesus said no one knows the day or the hour when He will return, not even the angels or Christ Himself! But He said when we see these endtime signs being fulfilled, we can know for a certainty that He is at the door...on the threshold of heaven...the angel has the trumpet of God to his mouth and is ready to signal His return.

Our major concern must not be the **signs** of His coming or in determining **when** He is coming. The one thing we have been commanded to do is to watch. Jesus said: *"But of that day and that hour knoweth no man, no, not the angels which are in heaven, neither the Son, but the Father. Take ye heed, **watch and pray**: for ye know not when the time is. For the Son of man is as a man taking a far journey, who left his house, and gave authority to his servants, and to every man his work, and commanded the porter to watch. **Watch** ye therefore; for ye know not when the master of the house cometh, at even, or at midnight, or at the cock crowing, or in the morning: Lest coming he find you sleeping. And what I say unto you I say unto all, **Watch**!"* (Mark 13:32-37).

The Greek word used in this verse for "watch" is "Agrupneo," which means not only keeping awake, but looking for and expecting something to happen.

Three times in these verses Jesus commanded the disciples to watch. He said, *"And what I say unto you, I say unto all, watch!" (Mark 13:37).* The Spirit of God is saying to the Church today:

Shake yourselves out of your sleep, My people! Why are you sleeping? Why are you resting and at ease? Do you not see the storm clouds gathering? Do you not hear My voice calling you to rise out of your sleep and out of your complacency?

Why do you close your eyes and take your rest when My coming is near, even at the door? I have chosen you and called you out as a people unto Myself. I have poured out My Spirit upon you and sent you forth to manifest My power and glory to the ends of the earth. Yet, you have become cumbered about with the cares of life. You have turned your heart away from Me saying, "It is not yet time." You have closed your eyes and your ears have become dulled from hearing My voice. Say no longer in your hearts, "There is yet time." For, behold, I am coming quickly.

It is time for My people to prepare. It is time for My people to rise out of their sleep and walk forward in My power and anointing to fulfill My will upon the earth. It is time for My people to warn the wicked of My judgments that are coming.

I am coming for those who are watching, who have on their garments of holiness and praise. Open your eyes, look around you and see that My coming is near. Hear My voice and heed My warning. *Arise, watch, prepare!*

Receive the Word of the Lord into your spirit!

To set a watch in prayer, the first step you must take is to shake yourself out of your sleep...not only must you be awake, you must keep awake.

There are many Christians today who are spiritually asleep. They are not aware of what the Spirit of God is doing upon the earth and are too busy living their lives as they please, seeking to fulfill their own wills, instead of doing the will of God.

There are Christians who have become sleepy...careless and unconcerned about the things of God and what is happening all around them. They have closed their eyes to the sin, pain and suffering around them.

Others have become cold and indifferent in their personal relationship with God. They no longer spend even five minutes a day in prayer or reading the Word of God.

In His messages to the seven churches, Jesus warned the Church in Sardis: *"Be watchful and strengthen the things which remain...if therefore thou shalt not watch, I will come on thee as a thief, and thou shalt not know what hour I come upon thee" (Revelation 3:2-3).*

Jesus' coming is going to be sudden...unexpected...without warning. He told His disciples, *"Be ye also ready: for in such an hour as ye think not the Son of man cometh" (Matthew 24:44).* He is going to come at a time when the world is not expecting Him.

Over and over He warned the seven churches in Revelation, *"Behold, I come quickly."* He told the Church in Ephesus, *"...repent and do the first works; or else I will come unto you quickly, and will remove thy candlestick out of his place..." (Revelation 2:5).*

He warned the Church in Pergamos, *"Repent; or else I will come unto thee quickly, and will fight against thee with the sword of my mouth" (Revelation 2:16).*

To the Church in Philadelphia, He said, *"Behold, I come quickly: hold that fast which thou hast that no man take thy crown" (Revelation 3:11).*

After revealing to John all the things which would be happening at His coming, He said, *"Behold, I come quickly; and my reward is with me, to give every man according as his work shall be" (Revelation 22:12).* His final warning was *"Surely I come quickly" (Revelation 22:20).*

Jesus warned that His coming would be suddenly, as a thief, to those who failed to watch. He said, *"If therefore thou shalt not watch, I will come on thee as a thief, and thou shalt not know what hour I come upon thee" (Revelation 3:3).* He said, *"Take ye heed, watch and pray:*

for ye know not when the time is" (Mark 13:33). **"Watch ye** *therefore: for ye know not when the master of the house cometh"* (Mark 13:35).

Paul told the Thessalonians: *"But of the times and the seasons, brethren, ye have no need that I write unto you. For yourselves know perfectly that* **the day of the Lord so cometh as a thief in the night***. For when they shall say, Peace and safety; then sudden destruction cometh upon them, as travail upon a woman with child; and they shall not escape" (I Thessalonians 5:1-3).*

To those who are not watching for Christ's return...who are spiritually asleep...who are unprepared, He is coming as a thief. His coming will catch them unaware and they will not be ready.

However, **He is not coming as a thief to those who are watching!** Paul said: *"But ye, brethren, are not in darkness, that that day should overtake you as a thief. Ye are all children of light and the children of the day: we are not of the night, nor of darkness" (I Thessalonians 5:4-5).*

You and I are not in spiritual darkness. By His Spirit, God has lifted the veil of darkness from our eyes and has revealed His endtime plan. We have seen the signs indicating His coming is even at the door. He has shown us the crises we are going to face. Now, we must make a decision that we are going to rise up in this final hour and set a watch in prayer! Paul said: *"Therefore, let us not sleep, as do others; but let us* **watch** *and be sober" (I Thessalonians 5:6).*

The Church as a whole has been asleep! We have become sidetracked from our real purpose. We have become comfortable and at ease.

Today we have a responsibility before God to be spiritually awake...alert...receptive to what the Spirit of God is saying. Knowing that we are living in the final hour before Christ's coming, we must be constantly awake, looking and expecting Him to return at any moment.

The second step you must take to set a watch in prayer, is to be constantly on guard.

Just as a soldier has been assigned to stand watch, we are to be constantly on guard and spiritually alert! We must guard ourselves and be looking for any sign of the enemy.

Like earthly soldiers, spiritual soldiers must be constantly on guard against enemy attack.

Just as in the natural a watch is set and the soldier is on guard for around-the-clock duty...24 hours a day...we must also set a watch in the spirit twenty-four hours a day. We must not let our guard down for one minute, under any circumstances!

One of the greatest dangers in the Church today is the deception many Christians are under that as long as they have "professed" themselves to be Christians, they will be caught up to meet Christ in the air when He comes. They have been deceived into thinking they can live haphazardly, following after the lusts of their flesh, following their own selfish will, living the way they please, and still make it into heaven.

Many Christians today have been deceived into thinking that they are prepared for Christ's coming. But they are not! Repeating the sinner's prayer, reading the Word, going to church, doing good works, paying tithes and offerings, does not mean that you are prepared and ready for Christ's coming.

When Christ returns, there will be many professing Christians who will not be able to enter the kingdom of Heaven. A separation is coming! The "chaff" is going to be separated from the "wheat." The "chaff" is not limited to the wicked and those who do not know Christ; the "chaff" is also the hypocrites, those claiming to be Christians but who, in reality, are not. The "chaff" is those Christians who are not living according to the Word and are not doing the will of God.

Jesus said: *"Not every one that saith unto me, Lord, Lord, shall enter into the kingdom of heaven;* ***but he that doeth the will of my Father which is in heaven"*** *(Matthew 7:21).*

Simply because an individual professes to be born again and claims Jesus as their Lord, that does not mean they belong to Him and are going to be welcomed into heaven.

Jesus said: *"Many will say to me in that day, Lord, Lord, have we not prophesied in thy name? And in thy name done many wonderful works? And then will I profess unto them, I never knew you: depart from me, ye that work iniquity"* *(Matthew 7:22-23).*

In these verses Jesus is not talking about wicked unbelievers. He is speaking of believers...so-called Christians... who are caught up in good works but are not walking in obedience...who have not fully surrendered their lives... who are not living according to God's will.

In His sermon on the Mount, Jesus told His disciples, *"And why call ye me, Lord, Lord, and* ***do not the things which I say?"*** *(Luke 6:46).* Those Christians who call Jesus "Lord" but fail or neglect to live according to the Word of God...and who reject and fail to do His will are hypocrites.

Jesus told them that those who hear His words and fail to do them are like a house without a foundation that is destroyed when the storms come. There are professing Christians today who read the Word...who hear sermon after sermon...yet they fail to practice what they hear. They have deceived themselves into thinking they are safe and secure, that they are ready to stand before God. But, like the house without a foundation, they will not be able to stand. They will not be able to enter into heaven.

Jesus said: ***"Strive*** *to enter in at the strait gate: for many,*

I say unto you, will seek to enter in, and shall not be able" (*Luke 13:24*).

Not everyone seeking to enter into heaven is going to make it. Jesus said to strive. The word "strive" in this verse is "agonizomai," which means "to contend, to labor fervently." Today is the day when we must spiritually strive…when we must be faithful not only in hearing the Word…when we must not only hear His voice…but obey it!

A day is soon coming when Christ is going to issue the command to His angels to gather His elect together from the four corners of the earth. *"And he shall send his angels with a great sound of a trumpet and they shall gather together his elect from the four winds, from one end of heaven to the other"* (*Matthew 24:31*). The chaff is going to be separated from the wheat. The elect…His endtime remnant is going to be caught up to meet Him in the air, and the door is going to be closed.

Jesus said: *"When once the master of the house is risen up, and hath shut the door, and ye begin to stand without, and to knock at the door, saying, Lord, Lord, open unto us; and he shall answer and say unto you, I know you not whence you are: Then shall ye begin to say, we have eaten and drunk in thy presence, and thou hast taught in our streets. But he shall say, I tell you, I know you not whence you are; depart from me, all ye workers of iniquity. There shall be weeping and gnashing of teeth, when ye shall see Abraham and Isaac and Jacob, and all the prophets of the kingdom of God, and you yourselves thrust out"* (*Luke 13:25-28*).

Let this picture sink deep into your spirit. On that great and final day when Christ returns and that final separation is made, there will be Christians saying, "We have sat in Your Presence, we have heard the Word preached, we have sat at Your table and tasted of Your goodness. Lord, open unto us!" But the door will be forever shut and they will be cast out into outer darkness where there is weeping and gnashing of teeth.

To Set A Watch, You Must Spiritually Strive To Enter Into Heaven!

Turn in your Bible to *Matthew, chapter 24, and read verses 36-51.* After Jesus had explained to His disciples the signs of His coming, He stressed upon them the importance of watching...preparing for His coming. He compared His coming to that of a householder who had left His servant in charge of caring for His estate. In these verses Jesus reveals the reward of His faithful servants and the terrible fate of those Christians who are unfaithful and are not ready when He returns.

Those Christians who are watching...prepared and faithful in doing His will when He returns, Christ will reward them and put them in charge of all His possessions.

Jesus said: *"Therefore keep watch because you do not know on what day your Lord will come. But understand this: If the owner of the house had known at what time of night the thief was coming, he would have kept watch and would not have let his house be broken into. So you also must be ready, because the Son of Man will come at an hour when you do not expect him"* (Matthew 24:42-44, NIV).

Jesus then asked the question: *"Who then is the faithful and wise servant, whom the master has put in charge of the servants in his household to give them their food at the proper time? It will be good for that servant whose master finds him **doing so** when he returns. I tell you the truth, he will put him in charge of all his possessions"* (Matthew 24:45-46, NIV).

The faithful servant is the one who is watching...in a constant state of readiness and expectancy. He is the one who is busy...not just hearing...not just talking...but doing the will of God regardless of what hour He comes.

On the other hand, the wicked servant is the one who is not ready but is taking his ease. Jesus said: *"But suppose that servant is wicked and says to himself, 'My master is staying away a long time,' and he then begins to beat his fellow servants and to eat and drink with drunkards. The master of that servant will come on a day when he does not expect him and at an hour he is not aware of. He will cut him to pieces and assign him a place **with the hypocrites**, where there will be weeping and gnashing of teeth"* (Matthew 24:48-51, NIV).

Jesus is not referring to wicked unbelievers in these verses. He is referring to the servants in His household... believers professing to be Christians. The reason the servant is considered wicked is because of his unbelief and unconcern regarding his master's coming. He is like the scoffers Peter said would come who would say, *"Where is the promise of his coming?" (II Peter 3:4)*. Because of this unconcern and his unwillingness to watch and be prepared, he is at ease, he fails to do the work his master has given him to do and becomes involved with all forms of ungodliness.

This is a warning to Christians. In *Matthew, chapter 25,* Jesus gives three more vivid examples...the parable of the ten virgins, the parable of the talents, and the parable of the sheep and the goats. These parables all clearly show that those Christians who are unfaithful in doing the will of God, who are not living in obedience to God's Word, who are not watching and ready for Christ's return, are not going to enter into heaven. The unfaithful servants are cast into the lake of fire along with the hypocrites!

To set a watch in prayer we must not only be spiritually alert and looking for Christ to return, we must be spiritually striving...diligently preparing ourselves for His coming. Jesus warned, *"Behold I come as a thief; blessed is he that* **watcheth***, and keepeth his garments, lest he walk naked, and they see his shame" (Revelation 16:15)*.

Do not be deceived. Jesus is coming for a pure bride... an endtime holy remnant...that is without spot or blemish. To set a watch, we must stay in a spiritual state of readiness where we are clothed in garments of holiness and righteousness.

Peter told the believers: *"But the day of the Lord will come as a thief in the night; in the which the heavens shall pass away with a great noise, and the elements shall melt with fervent heat, the earth also and the works that are therein shall be burned up. Seeing then that all these things shall be dissolved, what manner of persons ought ye to be in all holy conversation and godliness, Wherefore, beloved, seeing that ye look for such things, **be diligent** that ye may be found of him in peace, without spot and blameless" (II Peter 3:10-11, 14)*.

Knowing that when Christ comes there will be a final separation when He separates the chaff from the wheat...

Knowing He is coming for those who are ready, who are faithful and busy **doing** His will...

Knowing that not everyone who cries, "Lord, Lord" will enter into heaven...

We must spiritually strive...be diligent...be prepared... constantly busy fulfilling the will of God...guarding ourselves from anything that would hinder us from walking in holiness.

The third step you must take in setting a watch in prayer is to guard against becoming so weighted down with the cares of this life that Christ's coming will come upon you as a snare.

Jesus told His disciples: *"And take heed to yourselves, lest at any time your hearts be overcharged with surfeiting, and drunkenness, and* **cares of this life**, *and so that day come upon you unawares. For as a snare shall it come on all them that dwell on the face of the whole earth.* **Watch ye therefore, and pray always**, *that ye may be accounted worthy to escape all these things that shall come to pass, and to stand before the Son of man" (Luke 21:34-36).*

Jesus told the disciples to "take heed" to themselves. Instead of always pointing a finger or trying to set everyone else straight, in this final hour Christ is warning us to take heed...to take the mask off and take an honest look at ourselves. We need to strip ourselves of selfish pride...humble ourselves before God and allow Him to reveal to us anything in our lives that would hinder us from being prepared for Christ's coming.

The warning Christ gave in these verses is not to allow ourselves to become overcome by the temptations or cares of this life that the day of the Lord should catch us off guard. There are many Christians today who are at this point, who have become so burdened and loaded down with the down to earth...nitty gritty...cares of life they have become unaware of the lateness of the hour.

Many Christians have become so preoccupied with making a living, taking care of their families and enjoying the pleasures of this life that they are spiritually disabled. Their spiritual eyes...their discernment...has grown dim until they cannot discern the signs of Christ's coming. Their spiritual ears have grown dull until they are unable to hear what the Spirit of God is saying.

Jesus said His coming would be as a snare...a trap or a noose...upon all the earth. Knowing this danger of being caught unaware, we must set a watch in prayer...guard ourselves from setting our hearts upon material possessions and indulging and gratifying the lusts of our flesh.

Jesus said: *"Watch ye therefore, and pray always."* This is our command today!

Our purpose...

That we may be accounted worthy to escape...

That we will be able to stand before Christ at His appearing.

We must be faithful to watch and pray always so that we will be able to escape. This does not mean that we are going to escape in the sense that we will not have to endure or go through the crises that are coming upon the earth **before** Christ's return, but that when the judgments of God are being poured out upon the wicked, that we will be preserved and counted worthy to stand at Christ's coming.

We have been delivered from the **wrath** of God that Christ is going to pour out upon the wicked at His coming. Paul said, *"For God hath not appointed us to wrath, but to obtain salvation by our Lord Jesus Christ"* (I Thessalonians 5:9).

Not only must we set a watch in prayer so that we will be able to escape the judgments of God, but that we will also be able to **stand** before Christ at His coming...acquitted...holy...pure...blameless.

The prophet Malachi said, *"But who may abide the day of his coming? and who shall stand when he appeareth? for he is like a refiner's fire, and like fullers' soap"* (Malachi 3:2).

Most Christians today are more concerned about escaping than they are in being counted worthy to stand before Him. Our God is a consuming fire. Sinful flesh cannot stand in His Presence...it is devoured. He is altogether holy...nothing impure or unholy can stand before Him.

God wants you to set a watch in prayer...

1. So that you will not be unprepared at His coming...at ease and not busy doing His will.

2. So that you will not become entangled and burdened down by the cares of life and the day of the Lord come upon you as a snare.

3. So that you will not be deceived during the wave of deception sweeping across the earth.

4. So that you will be prepared to face and overcome during the coming crises.

5. So that you will escape the judgments of God and be able to stand before Christ at His coming.

God Is Commissioning You To Set A Watch In Constant Prayer...24 Hours A Day!

Jesus said, *"Watch ye therefore, and **pray always**..."* *(Luke 21:36).* Watching and praying must go together. God is calling the Church to intensify their prayers to a level greater than ever before in its history. It is no longer a matter of choice; it is a matter of survival! It will make the difference between walking in victory and living in defeat. Those Christians who want to escape God's wrath and be able to stand before Christ, must make prayer a constant practice in their lives.

Knowing the crises that are coming in the nineties, there is no alternative. The Body of Christ must rise up out of its complacency and set a watch in prayer. The children of this world are wiser in their generation than we are. When they know of danger approaching, they will keep awake and stand on their guard against it.

In the Church today the average Christian does not spend even five minutes in prayer each day. Think about it! While thousands of New Age believers are "meditating" and communicating with demon spirits, the Church has become too preoccupied with other things. Christians today spend more time socializing than they do praying together.

Where are the all-night prayer meetings where the saints of God travailed and agonized in prayer until the fire of God fell from heaven and revival swept through the Church?

The type of prayer God is calling the Church to today is not a matter of setting a specific time each day for prayer and going through some set formula. It is not a short five- or ten-minute prayer said hurriedly before falling into bed. It is not thirty minutes, or even one hour in prayer each day.

To **set a watch** means around the clock duty...twenty-four hours a day. Jesus said, *"Watch ye therefore, and pray always" (Luke 21:36)*. The type of prayer God is calling the Body of Christ to today is constant prayer twenty-four hours a day.

You may be wondering, "How is that going to be possible?" God is calling us to be spiritually alert and remain in a constant attitude of prayer and communion with Him. In addition to special times of deep intercessory prayer, we must keep our hearts and minds...our thoughts...desires... and the meditations of our hearts centered upon God. Throughout the day we must offer up prayer and thanksgiving...on the job...at school...driving in the car...at home...whatever we may be doing.

Knowing a crisis is coming to the family, be continually in prayer throughout the day for your husband, wife, children and unsaved loved ones.

Knowing we are going to face a crisis of satanic confrontation, where we are in direct confrontation with Satan and his demons, you must remain in an attitude of prayer where you are spiritually alert and prepared to defeat the enemy.

God is calling members of the Body of Christ into a new, stronger spiritual bond in prayer. In addition to putting on the whole armor of God every day, Paul said we are to **pray always for all saints**.

He said: *"Praying always with all prayer and supplication in the Spirit, and watching thereunto with all perseverance and supplication for all saints" (Ephesians 6:18)*.

As the Body of Christ comes together in unity of the Spirit, in a close covenant relationship with one another, God is calling us to set a watch by persevering in prayer for members of the Body of Christ around the world.

We must begin to function as one Body...lifting up the needs of our brothers and sisters in need in our cities, communities and the nations of the world. We must not limit our prayers to those Christians within our local congregations, but we must be aware of the needs of the Body of

Christ in various parts of the world and continually persevere in prayer on their behalf.

God is looking for true warriors today who will come before Him with a pure heart to stand in the gap on behalf of the Body of Christ and their nations so that we may see restoration.

The prophet Daniel was given a revelation of the hour in which he lived and the crises the nation of Israel faced. He went into God's throne room with this revelation of what God was going to do and stood in the gap for the people of Israel.

Daniel said, *"And I set my face unto the Lord God to seek by prayer and supplications with fasting, and sackcloth and ashes" (Daniel 9:3).* He cried out to God, confessing the sins of the people. *"O Lord, hear; O Lord, forgive; O Lord, hearken and do; defer not, for thine own sake, O my God: for thy city and thy people are called by thy name" (Daniel 9:19).*

The same is true with us today. God has given us a revelation of the lateness of the hour and the crises that are coming in the decade of the nineties. Like Daniel, we must set our face and go before God in seasons of prayer and fasting, confessing our sins, the sins of the Church and our nation, and praying for a revival of repentance and restoration.

It is time for God's people to sound the alarm and get on their faces before God in prayer.

The prophet Joel declared: *"Blow ye the trumpet in Zion, and sound an alarm, in my holy mountain: let all the inhabitants of the land tremble: for the day of the LORD cometh, for it is nigh at hand" (Joel 2:1).*

This is not a time for us to be at ease. There is no time for us to sit back, fold our hands and relax. God is calling us to a solemn assembly. The day of the Lord is at hand Joel said, *"Gird yourselves, and lament, ye priests:* **howl***, ye ministers of the altar: come, lie all night in sackcloth, ye ministers of my God" (Joel 1:13).*

He said, *"Let the priests, the ministers of the LORD weep between the porch and the altar..." (Joel 2:17).*

The Lord is saying to us today, *"...turn ye even to me with all your heart, and with fasting, and with weeping, and with mourning" (Joel 2:12).*

This is the message of the hour! God is calling His people to set a watch in prayer. This is the strategy we must use today to be victorious during the coming crises. Before restoration comes to the Body of Christ, there must come a time of true repentance and intercession. There is no other way!

I urge you, with all that is within me, hear what the Spirit of God is saying and begin today...this very hour...to set a watch in prayer.

Chapter 8

Wave 1: A New Wave Of Holiness!

Just as the Body of Christ is facing the Five Major Crises I have revealed to you that are coming in the nineties, we are also going to see the greatest outpouring and manifestation of God's Spirit that the Church has ever known!

God has given us the prophecy:

"A powerful spiritual force is about to be released within the Body of Christ that will bring about the greatest manifestation of the power of God the world has ever seen..."

There is coming a great endtime outpouring of the Holy Spirit that is far greater than anything we have ever experienced. The world is going to see a manifestation of the supernatural power of God through miracles, signs and wonders that is going to be a mighty endtime witness that He is the all-powerful Lord God Jehovah and that He is the one true and living God!

The Holy Spirit is going to sweep across the face of this earth into every nation, every tribe and every tongue. Joel prophesied there would be a great endtime outpouring of God's Spirit upon all flesh before the great day of the Lord. He said: *"And it shall come to pass afterward, that I will pour out my spirit upon all flesh; and your sons and your daughters shall prophesy, your old men shall dream dreams, your young men shall see visions: And also upon the servants and upon the handmaids in those days will I pour out my spirit. And I will shew wonders in the heavens and in the earth, blood, and fire, and pillars of smoke. The sun shall be turned into darkness, and the moon into blood, before the great and the terrible day of the Lord come. And it shall come to pass, that whosoever shall call on the name of the Lord shall be delivered: for in mount Zion and in Jerusalem shall be deliverance, as the Lord hath said, and in the remnant whom the Lord shall call." (Joel 2:28-32).*

Since the Day of Pentecost, when the Holy Spirit swept through the upper room as a mighty, rushing wind, empowering the Church to fulfill the Great Commission, there have been various moves or waves of the Holy Spirit. At the turn of the century, in the early 1900s, there was a powerful wave of the Holy Spirit during the Azusa Street Revival which began in Los Angeles, California. Then in the early 1970s, there was another wave of the Holy Spirit, referred to as the "Charismatic" revival, that came sweeping through the Church. Denominational barriers were broken as Catholics, Baptists, Episcopalians, Presbyterians and people of all denominations were baptized in the Holy Spirit, with the accompanying sign of speaking in unknown tongues.

Today, as we enter the decade of the nineties, we are going to experience a mighty endtime outpouring of the Holy Spirit unlike any other and greater in scope and dimension. The dramatic changes that are now taking place behind the Iron and Bamboo Curtains are opening doors for a short period of time, during which there will be an opportunity for the Body of Christ to spread the Gospel in Russia, China and other nations which have been previously closed.

Joel prophesied that God's Spirit would be poured out upon **all** flesh. Nothing can stop this endtime outpouring! Communism cannot stop it. The Iron Curtain...Bamboo Curtain...Satan and all his demonic forces cannot stop what God is going to do in this endtime harvest. Satan will be doing everything he can to hinder it. He will be warring against God's people, but he will not stop this final endtime outpouring of God's Spirit.

Concerning this endtime outpouring of the Holy Spirit, Joel said, *"And it shall come to pass afterward, that I will pour out my spirit upon all flesh" (Joel 2:28)*. Circle the word "afterward." What was he referring to when he said "afterward"? The entire book of Joel was written concerning the coming day of the Lord. He said, *"Alas for the day! for the day of the Lord is at hand" (Joel 1:15). "...let all the in-habitants of the land tremble: for the day of the Lord cometh, for it is nigh at hand" (Joel 2:1). "...for the day of the Lord is great and very terrible; and who can abide it?" (Joel 2:11).*

In the previous chapters, the Lord is calling His people to fasting and prayer...to a time of repentance.

He said, *"...turn ye even to me with all your heart, and with fasting, and with weeping and with mourning: And rend your heart, and not your garments, and turn unto the Lord your God" (Joel 2:12-13).*

The Lord calls His ministers to weep and to cry out to God on behalf of the people. He said, *"Let the priests, the ministers of the Lord, weep between the porch and the altar, and let them say, Spare thy people, O Lord, and give not thine heritage to reproach..." (Joel 2:17).*

After this time of prayer and repentance comes the promised restoration and endtime outpouring. Joel said, *"Then will the Lord be jealous for his land, and pity his people" (Joel 2:18).* He said, *"And it shall come to pass afterward that I will pour out my spirit upon all flesh" (Joel 2:28).*

Every major wave of the Holy Spirit has been preceded by a time of prayer. The outpouring of the Holy Spirit on the Day of Pentecost came as 120 believers were in the upper room praying together in one accord. The great Azusa Street Revival started when a small handful of believers came together in one accord to pray for revival.

Today, God is calling His people into an "Upper Room" experience, where we will stay on our faces before Him in repentance and intercession for the Body of Christ until we see the promised endtime outpouring of His Spirit.

One of the major strategies Satan is using today to stop the Church from entering into the dimension of power and authority God has planned for it, is to use every possible tactic to keep the Church from praying. His objective is to keep you so busy and worn out with the cares of this life, until you think you don't have time to pray.

Satan and his demons cannot stand it when God's people get in earnest before God and persevere in prayer!

Don't kid yourself! Satan knows the power of prayer. He

doesn't mind the Church becoming involved in all types of various ministries and outreaches, social functions and even Bible studies, because without a solid foundation of prayer there is no power or anointing of God behind our good works to meet the great needs the world is facing today. But the moment Satan sees God's people dedicate themselves to fasting and prayer, he gets scared. He gets mad and sends his demon spirits to create confusion, to hinder, to create a diversion or try to stop them from praying.

If there was ever a time when God's people need to unite together in prayer, it is today! It is my prayer that you received the commission God has given us to set a watch in prayer, and that you have made a new dedication to prayer.

Before the Body of Christ can experience restoration and this endtime outpouring, there must first come a time of repentance. There are no shortcuts. God's power is released through us as we pray! Our strength to face the coming crises and to fulfill His purpose for us in this endtime harvest is going to come only through prayer.

The purpose for this endtime outpouring of His Spirit is...

1. To prepare us for Christ's Coming.
2. To empower the Body of Christ to fulfill this endtime spiritual destiny.
3. To bring in a great harvest of souls.
4. To manifest God's power and glory as a final endtime witness to the nations of the world.

Wave 1
In the decade of the nineties, God has shown me there is coming to the Body of Christ...

A New Wave Of True Holiness!
A spirit of true holiness, righteousness and consecration on a new level is coming to the Body of Christ to prepare us for Christ's coming. There will be no more compromise or hypocrisy. Emotionalism will be replaced by serious dedication.

Do not be deceived! Jesus is not coming to receive a harlot bride that is committing spiritual adultery with the world. He is not coming for a bride that has become polluted with the sinful lusts and desires of this world. He is coming for a holy endtime remnant...a people who have been cleansed and purified...without spot or blemish.

Jesus came to earth, suffered the shame and agony of the cross, died and was resurrected that we would be holy and without blemish. Paul said concerning Christ and the Church, *"Husbands, love your wives, even as Christ also loved the Church and gave himself for it. That he might sanctify and cleanse it with the washing of the water by the word,* **That he might present it to himself a glorious church, not having spot, or wrinkle or any such thing; but that it should be holy and without blemish** *"* *(Ephesians 5:25-27).*

We are living in the greatest time of promiscuousness and evil since Sodom and Gomorrah! Jesus said that one of the signs before His coming would be that sin would abound! He said, *"And because iniquity shall abound, the love of many shall wax cold" (Matthew 24:12).*

We are living in the time of great deception and apostasy in the church. Paul warned Timothy about when *"evil men and seducers shall wax worse and worse, deceiving, and being deceived" (II Timothy 3:13).*

In this evil generation God has chosen and called us out from the world to walk in holiness before Him. We are commanded by God to be holy even as He is holy. *"But as he which hath called you is holy, so be ye holy in all manner of conversation; Because it is written, Be ye holy; for I am holy" (I Peter 1:15-16).* Through the blood of Jesus, He has made it possible for us to be clothed with Christ's righteousness and to live a life that is holy and blameless before Him.

God has planned for us to set a standard of **holiness for the world**.

Paul told the Philippians: *"...Show yourselves to be blameless and guileless, innocent and uncontaminated children of God without blemish (faultless, unrebukable) in the midst of a crooked and wicked generation–(spiritually) perverted and perverse. Among whom you are seen as bright lights–stars or beacons shining out clearly–in the (dark) world;" (Philippians 2:15, TAB).*

However, instead of following God's standard of holiness, the Church has become polluted by the world. Instead of speaking out and rebuking the sin that surrounds us, the Church has compromised with the world and has become comfortable with the sin that surrounds it!

When we take the mask off and take an honest look at the Church today, we can see that sin has so infiltrated the Church that it is difficult to distinguish Christians from the world. The Church is full of hypocrites...so-called Christians who are professing to live a holy life but who are fulfilling the lusts of their flesh.

There are those professing to be Christians who go to church, dance, shout and praise the Lord, but the minute they walk out the door they begin to spread gossip, criticize and tear down the pastor or other members of the Body of Christ.

There are men and women who are bound by lust and who are involved in adulterous relationships, yet see nothing wrong with it. They feel they can continue illicit relationships and still be Christians.

There are so-called Christians today who think nothing of lying, stealing or cheating on their jobs. They take days off and call in sick, take supplies home from the office, take extra time at coffee breaks and extend their lunch hours.

There are Christian businessmen who think nothing of lying or cheating on their income taxes, who cheat their customers, who purposely misrepresent the facts, who become involved in questionable business deals with unbelievers.

There are Christians who allow their hearts and minds to be filled with all sorts of evil imaginations and fantasies. They watch R-rated movies, filled with foul language, sex and violence. They tell dirty jokes on the job, read cheap romance novels and watch "soaps" on television.

In many churches today worldliness is no longer condemned but is encouraged through doctrines that are being preached which cause Christians to set their affections on the things of this world and teach them to seek after material possessions.

There are men and women filling our churches today who outwardly appear to be righteous, who have a form of godli-

In many churches today, members are actually encouraged to set their affections on the wealth of the world.

ness, but who are filled with hatred, bitterness, unforgive-ness, pride, greed, jealousy and other ungodly attitudes.

The Word of God teaches we are to deny ungodliness and worldly lusts. Paul told Titus, *"For the grace of God that bringeth salvation hath appeared to all men,* ***Teaching us that, denying ungodliness and worldly lusts, we should live soberly, righteously, and godly, in this present world"*** *(Titus 2:11-12).*

Peter told the believer, *"Therefore, rid yourselves of all malice, and all deceit,* ***hypocrisy****, envy, and slander of every kind"* *(I Peter 2:1, NIV).*

The Word of God teaches us that we are not to love the world or the things that are in this world. *"Love not the world, neither the things that are in the world. If any love the world, the love of the Father is not in him"* *(I John 2:15).*

When we lust after the material possessions of this world and its pleasures, we are committing spiritual adultery. James warned the believers, *"Ye adulterers and adulter-esses, know ye not that the friendship of the world is in en-mity with God? Whosoever therefore will be a friend of the world is the enemy of God"* *(James 4:4).*

In the church today we no longer hear sermons preached on self-denial, crucifixion of self or separation from the world. They are not popular. People do not want to hear that they must die to self and to the world. Instead of sermons on holiness, dedication and consecration, ministers are preaching and teaching what people want to hear...how to be successful...self-fulfillment...how to prosper and use your faith and the Word to obtain worldly possessions.

In the decade of the nineties, we will see a growing apostasy within the Church. As persecution comes, there will be those who will compromise with the world rather than endure persecution for the Gospel. There are those who will be deceived and will turn away from the faith.

In the decade of the nineties, as the Church continues to become polluted through compromise and sin, there will be a separation between the ungodly compromisers and the true saints of God who are walking before Him in holiness.

God Is Calling Us To Separate Ourselves From The Apostate Church And The World!

In his vision of the endtimes, the apostle John saw the corrupt apostate church and heard a voice from heaven, saying: *"Come out of her, my people, that ye be not partakers of her sins, and that ye receive not of her plagues. For her sins have reached unto heaven, and God hath remembered her iniquities" (Revelation 18:4-5).*

During this wave of true holiness and righteousness that is coming to the Church, God is calling us to separate ourselves from the apostate church and the world. Not only are we to put to death our worldly desires and lusts of the flesh, we must sever ourselves completely from relationships with unbelievers and **Christians who are compromising with the world and are not living according to the Word.**

Paul told the Thessalonians: *"Now we charge you, brethren, in the name and on the authority of our Lord Jesus Christ, the Messiah, that you withdraw and keep away from every brother (fellow believer) who is slack in the performance of duty and is disorderly, living as a shirker and not walking in accord with the traditions and instructions that you have received from us" (II Thessalonians 3:6, TAB).*

He told the Ephesians: *"But among you there must not be even a hint of sexual immorality, or of any kind of impurity, or of greed, because these are improper for God's holy people. Nor should there be obscenity, foolish talk or coarse joking, which are out of place, but rather thanksgiving. For of this you can be sure: No immoral, impure or greedy person —such a man is an idolator—has any inheritance in the kingdom of Christ and of God. Let no one deceive you with empty words, for because of such things God's wrath comes on those who are disobedient. **Therefore do not be partners with them**"* (*Ephesians 5:3-7, NIV*).

He told the Corinthians: *"I wrote you in my letter not to associate with immoral people; I did not at all mean with the immoral people of this world, or with the covetous and swindlers, or with idolaters; for then you would have to go out of the world. But actually, I wrote to you not to associate with any so-called brother if he should be an immoral person, or covetous, or an idolater, or a reviler, or a drunkard, or a swindler-**not even to eat with such a one**"* (*I Corinthians 5:9-11, NAS*).

God does not want us to develop or maintain relationships with Christians who are immoral, worldly minded, greedy, or who use foul language. Paul said, *"And have no fellowship with the unfruitful works of darkness, but rather reprove them"* (*Ephesians 5:11*).

As we prepare for Christ's coming, God is calling us to a deeper level of holiness and consecration than ever before. We must separate ourselves and sever any relationships with Christians who are walking contrary to the Word of God. As long as we maintain these relationships, we are in a weakened spiritual condition and are giving Satan an opportunity to attack and lead us into compromise.

In this new Wave of Holiness, God is saying, "Come out from among them and be ye separate." To enter into this new dimension of holiness may mean that you will have to break off relationships and close fellowship and communion with friends or loved ones.

This will not be easy, but you must be willing to do it if you want to be part of that endtime holy remnant...that pure and spotless bride that Christ is preparing for Himself.

Not only must we separate ourselves from so-called Christians who are living ungodly, unworldly lives, we must not be unequally yoked together with unbelievers. There must not be any fellowship, communion or agreement made with unbelievers. Paul told the believers in the Corinthian church: *"Do not be bound together with unbelievers; for what partnership have righteousness and lawlessness, or what fellowship has light with darkness? Or what harmony has Christ with Belial, or what has a believer in common with an unbeliever? Or what agreement has the temple of God with idols? For we are the temple of the living God; just as God said, "I will dwell in them and walk among them; and I will be their God, and they shall be my people. **Therefore, come out from their midst and be separate**,"* says the Lord, *"**and do not touch what is unclean**;" (II Corinthians 6:14-17, NAS).*

The Word of God is clear. God does not want us to join ourselves together in close communion and have intimate fellowship with unbelievers. There are Christians today who have formed social and business relationships and partnerships with unbelievers. God is saying, "Come ye out from them and be ye separate!"

Christians who form close business relationships and partnerships with unbelievers are going contrary to the Word of God. They are exposing themselves to worldliness and have entered into friendship with the world.

Friendship with the world is *"enmity against God"* *(James 4:4).* The moment you enter into such a relationship with unbelievers, whether it be a business relationship or a close personal relationship, you become the enemy of God. *"Whosoever therefore will be a friend of the world is the enemy of God" (James 4:4).* It is spiritual adultery

During this coming wave of holiness and righteousness, Christians must be willing to sever business relationships with unbelievers, even if it means a financial loss. Christians are going to have to break off from worldly friendships and intimate association with unbelievers…friends…relatives… co-workers. This does not mean that God is telling us to turn our backs on them or have nothing to do with them at all.

We must pray for them, reprove their works of darkness and warn them of coming judgment and God's wrath that is going to be poured out upon the wicked. But we cannot walk in close fellowship with them.

God does not want us to make unholy alliances with the world. "Unholy alliances" are any type of linking together with the world. When Christians rent video tapes at a video store that also has X-rated videos or videos on witchcraft or the occult, they are supporting that video store with their money and it is an "unholy alliance."

When a Christian works in a book store or store that has books on the occult, promotes New Age teaching, sells Playboy magazines and other pornographic literature, it is an "unholy alliance."

When churches or Christians make property or business investments in worldly businesses or organizations that sell alcoholic beverages, pornographic literature or promote worldly entertainment and worldly attitudes, it is an "unholy alliance."

We must guard against making any "unholy alliances." If you have built a close relationship or partnership with unbelievers, break it. Don't place yourself in a position where you may become polluted by the world and its worldly attitudes.

This separation and new dimension of holiness is going to be necessary if we are going to be able to stand before Christ at His coming. Peter said, *"Beloved, seeing that ye look for such things,* **be diligent** *that ye may be found of him in peace, without spot, and blameless" (II Peter 3:14).*

Jesus has warned us to take heed...to watch and pray always that we *"may be accounted worthy to escape all these things that shall come to pass, and* **to stand before the Son of man** *" (Luke 21:36).*

Jesus said, *"Behold, I come as a thief. Blessed is he that watcheth, and* **keepeth his garments***, lest he walk naked, and they see his shame" (Revelation 16:15).* Christ's message to the lukewarm church members, with one foot in the world and one foot in the church, is: *"I counsel thee to buy of me gold tried in the fire, that thou mayest be rich; and white raiment that thou mayest be clothed and that the shame of thy nakedness do not appear..." (Revelation 3:18).*

Do you want to be able to **stand** before Christ at His coming?

Only those who are clothed in His righteousness, who have on their wedding garments of holiness...without spot or blemish...are going to be able to stand before Him.

Many Christians today, when they think of a great move of the Spirit, think of the outward manifestation. They associate an outpouring of His Spirit with people shouting, singing, dancing in the Spirit and rejoicing. These outward expressions of the moving of God's Spirit are good. There is nothing wrong with them.

However, this coming Wave of True Holiness that is coming goes much deeper...beyond emotionalism. It is going to be a deep inner working where Christ will do some deep cleaning in our lives to prepare us for His coming.

Christians who are only looking for the outward manifestations...the power and glory...instead of looking to the Lord and asking Him to purge out the sin in their lives... will not even recognize this great move of the Spirit when it comes.

During this wave of the Holy Spirit, a spirit of righteousness is coming upon God's people who want to walk in true holiness. As it comes upon us, it will replace mere "emotionalism" with a serious dedication and consecration.

In the decade of the nineties a time of cleansing and purging is coming to the Body of Christ! God's people are going to be tried as gold is tried in the fire, until all the impurities...everything in our lives that is unholy and displeasing to Him...is burned up.

This time of purging will not be easy. It will be painful. God is going to allow circumstances to come into our lives that will bring to the surface the hidden attitudes of our hearts, the impurities, the worldly attitudes, unholy thoughts and unholy actions.

Malachi prophesied: *"But who may abide the day of his coming? and who shall stand when he appeareth? for he is like a refiner's fire and like fullers' soap: And he shall sit as a refiner and purifier of silver: and he shall purify the sons of Levi, and purge them as gold and silver, that they may offer unto the Lord an offering in righteousness" (Malachi 3:2-3).*

In his vision of the endtimes, the Lord spoke to Daniel

saying, *"Go thy way, Daniel: for the words are closed up and sealed till the time of the end. Many shall be purified, and made white, and tried"* (Daniel 12:9-10).

Before Christ returns, He is going to purge...to cleanse the Body of Christ. John the Baptist said concerning Christ: *"...he shall baptize you with the Holy Ghost and with fire: Whose fan is in his hand, and he will thoroughly purge his floor, and gather his wheat into the garner; but he will burn up the chaff with unquenchable fire"* (Matthew 3:11-12).

During this time of spiritual cleansing, when the Lord begins to purge...to strip away our self-righteousness and pride and expose the sin in our lives, as we humble ourselves before God, yield to this purging and rid ourselves of the things He reveals to us, we will begin to walk in true holiness in every aspect of our lives.

As a result of coming into this new relationship with Christ...of drawing near to Him and allowing Him to cleanse us...there will be a manifestation of true holiness...not a form or doctrine...but the real thing.

No more hypocrisy...saying one thing and doing another. There will be a genuine manifestation of holiness in our conversation, in our thoughts, in our attitudes, and in all our relationships.

To be part of this Wave of the Holy Spirit, you must, first of all, cry out to God and ask Him to take the spiritual "blinders" off your eyes. Humble yourself before Him and ask Him to expose all sin in your life that may be hidden to you.

You must be willing to submit yourself to Christ and allow Him to cut away all those things that are ungodly and unholy in His sight. Don't try to measure yourself with the world's standards, or by the standards man has set. The Lord has commanded us, *"Be ye holy for I am holy"* (I Peter 1:16). We are to be holy as He is holy! We are to be partakers of His holiness (Hebrews 12:10).

As Christ exposes the sin and unrighteousness in your life, you must get rid of it!` If you have formed "unholy alliances" with the world, break them.

If Christ reveals to you jealousy, hatred, bitterness or other ungodly attitudes, take authority over them and get them out of your heart.

If you have allowed worldliness and the lusts of your flesh to gain a hold in your life, submit yourself to the Lord and ask Him to cleanse you of all worldly desires.

Peter said, *"Beloved, seeing that ye look for such things,* **be diligent** *that ye may be found of him in peace, without spot and blameless" (II Peter 3:14).* Be diligent! We must spiritually strive! Jesus said, *"Strive to enter in at the strait gate" (Luke 13:24).*

Paul said to follow after holiness *"...without which no man shall see the Lord: Looking diligently lest any man fail of the grace of God" (Hebrews 12:14-15).* This means we are to seek after holiness...to continually come before the Lord and allow Him to reveal the sin and impurities in our lives. Then we must draw upon the Holy Spirit to continually bring our bodies into submission to Him and His Word.

Paul said, *"But (like a boxer) I buffet my body—handle it roughly, discipline it by hardships and subdue it—for fear that after proclaiming to others the Gospel and things pertaining to it, I myself should become unfit—not stand the test and be unapproved—and rejected (as a counterfeit)" I Corinthians 9:27, TAB).*

Walk in an attitude of submission and repentance before God. You must bring your body into submission to the Word of God and perfect holiness in the fear of God.

Paul told the Corinthians: *"Having therefore these promises, dearly beloved,* **let us cleanse ourselves from all filthiness of the flesh and spirit, perfecting holiness in the fear of God**" *(II Corinthians 7:1).*

This Wave of True Holiness is coming to the Body of Christ. To be able to stand before Christ at His coming, pure...holy...without spot or blemish...clothed in His righteousness...you must allow Christ to purge and cleanse you now!

Hear what the Spirit of the Lord is saying and begin now to prepare yourself for this great wave of the Holy Spirit that is coming to the Church.

Chapter 9

Wave 2: Great Signs, Wonders And Miracles

We are on the verge of experiencing the greatest endtime manifestation of God's supernatural signs, wonders and miracles that this world has ever known!

In the decade of the nineties, a new Wave of the Holy Spirit is coming to the true Body of Christ that will bring us to a **full manifestation** of the power and glory of God.

Remember the prophecy God has given us:

"A powerful spiritual force is about to be released within the Body of Christ that will bring about the greatest manifestation of the power of God the world has ever seen..."

As the Body of Christ is brought through the fire... purged and cleansed...and we are walking in true holiness before God, the supernatural power of God is going to be released through us in an even greater dimension than that of the Early Church.

We will no longer look back to the great signs and wonders God manifested through Israel or the Early Church and wonder why we are not seeing them manifested through us.

For years I have been prophesying to you that the Church is going to be raptured in a greater demonstration of power than it was born in. We are now entering into a period of time when God is going to manifest great signs and wonders through the **true** Body of Christ that will be an even greater manifestation to the world than during the ministry of the Early Church.

The second major Wave of the Holy Spirit God has shown me is coming in the decade of the nineties is...

A New Wave of Signs, Wonders and Miracles

A powerful spiritual force is coming to the Church in a

manifestation of signs, wonders and miracles that will give the Church a divine capability to confront Satan's demon forces and Satan himself.

Christians will rise up with a new authority! We will not shrink back from the enemy, but will stand up to the powers of the enemy...not just in the broad-brush term, but in direct confrontation. There will be a new boldness and fearlessness.

The identity of the actual satanic powers that are over our cities will be made manifest so that we will be able to fight against Satan and his demons in direct confrontation and not just deal with them in generalities.

During this new Wave of Signs, Wonders and Miracles:

There will be a great endtime harvest of souls with multiplied thousands of people around the world, in every nation, being saved and filled with the Holy Spirit. As doors open in Russia, China, Japan and other countries that have been previously closed to the Gospel, the Spirit of God is going to be poured out.

God has promised, *"And it shall come to pass afterward, that I will pour out my spirit upon all flesh"* (Joel 2:28). The Hebrew word for "pour" is "shaphak, which means "to spill forth or gush out." The Spirit of God is going to gush forth until it covers the earth and accomplishes the purposes of God.

We will see an increase in manifestations of the gifts of the Spirit. As members of the Body of Christ begin to walk in true holiness before God, they will prophesy, have spiritual dreams and visions. The Body of Christ will begin to flow in the gifts of the Spirit.

We will see creative miracles and mass healings, where entire congregations will be healed.

We will experience miracles of God's supernatural provision, where God will supernaturally provide food, clothing, divine protection and deliverance from the enemy.

We will see supernatural signs and wonders on earth and in the heavens.

God spoke through Joel: *"And I will show wonders in the heavens and in the earth, blood, and fire, and pillars of smoke. The sun shall be turned into darkness, and the moon into blood,* **before the great and the terrible** *day of the LORD come." (Joel 2:30-31).*

Jesus told His disciples: *"And there shall be signs in the sun, and in the moon, and in the stars; and upon the earth distress of nations, with perplexity; the sea and the waves roaring; Men's hearts failing them for fear, and for looking after those things which are coming on the earth: for the powers of heaven shall be shaken. And then shall they see the Son of man coming in a cloud with power and great glory " (Luke 21:25-27).*

"Immediately after the tribulation of those days shall the sun be darkened, and the moon shall not give her light, and the stars shall fall from heaven, and the powers of the heavens shall be shaken. And then shall appear the sign of the Son of man in heaven: And then *shall all the tribes of the earth mourn, and they shall see the Son of man coming in the clouds of heaven with power and great glory. And he shall send his angels with a great sound of a trumpet, and they shall gather together* **his elect** *from the four winds, from one end of heaven to the other" (Matthew 24:29-31).*

The purpose of this endtime outpouring, this wave of Signs, Wonders and Miracles is not for show. It is not just so we can attend church services and special meetings, see the miracles of God being manifested in our midst, and praise God, and then go home and live our daily lives in the natural realm.

God wants us **to walk** in the supernatural! He wants us to look to God for His supernatural provision in our daily lives...in providing food, clothing, shelter, transportation. He wants us to depend upon Him for supernatural protection, for guidance, health, our finances, and for all our needs.

However, God does not want us to get our eyes so centered upon the **outward manifestation** of miracles taking place that we fail to understand God's purpose for pouring out His Spirit upon us in this endtime harvest before Christ's return.

God's purpose for this Wave of Signs, Wonders and Miracles is:

1. To empower the Body of Christ to fulfill endtime spiritual destiny.

2. To give us the divine capability and power through the Holy Spirit to have direct confrontation with Satan and his demons.

3. To bring in a harvest of souls.

4. To manifest God's supernatural power as a final end-time witness to the nations of the world.

God is a God of plan, purpose, design and objectivity. He is not going to pour out His power and manifest His signs and wonders in our midst just so we will be able to rejoice, shout, dance and praise God.

We are a people of spiritual destiny! In these final moments of time before Christ's coming, He has given us an awesome responsibility!

The Gospel is to be preached throughout the nations of the earth before Christ returns.

Jesus said: *"And this gospel of the kingdom shall be preached in all the world **for a witness** unto all nations; **and then shall the end come** " (Matthew 24:14).*

The world is going to have a final endtime witness of the Gospel of Jesus Christ...not just the preaching of the written word...but the resurrection message of Jesus Christ is going to be preached in a demonstration of the supernatural power of God with accompanying miracles, signs and wonders as living proof that Jesus is Who He claims to be...the Son of the living God!

In John's vision of the endtimes, he saw an angel flying through the heavens with the Gospel to preach to the nations of the earth.

John said: *"And I saw another angel fly in the midst of heaven, having the everlasting gospel to preach unto them that dwell on the earth, and to every nation, and kindred, and tongue, and people, Saying with a loud voice, Fear God, and give glory to him; for the hour of his judgment is come: and worship him that made heaven, and earth, and the sea, and the fountains of waters" (Revelation 14:6-7).*

This angel preaching the Gospel represents an endtime move of world evangelization that will take place before Christ's return. This endtime worldwide evangelism will not only be accomplished by mass evangelistic crusades or through the preaching of well-known evangelists alone. We are going to see technological breakthroughs and new opportunities through satellite technology that will enable us to go into areas never before reached by the Gospel, and we will be able to multiply the number of people that we reach many times over.

However, this is not the major method that is going to be used to get the job done. We are entering a new era of evangelism, where the work is going to be accomplished through one-on-one evangelism! During this Wave of Signs, Wonders and Miracles, God is going to pour out His Spirit upon the true Body of Christ.

A powerful spiritual force will be released, giving members of the Body a new strength, a new authority, and a divine capability to be His endtime witnesses throughout the nations of the earth.

The Body of Christ is going to rise up in the power and anointing of the Holy Spirit to proclaim the Gospel of Jesus Christ on their jobs...in their neighborhoods...in the communities...on the streets...at the market...everywhere we go!

We will not be preaching a watered-down, compromising message to tickle people's ears. We will be preaching the message of Jesus Christ in a demonstration of the supernatural power of Almighty God. We will not just be **talking** about God's miracle power to save, heal, deliver from drugs, alcohol and all the power of the enemy. God will be confirming what we say with signs following, as He did in the early Church.

The members of the early Church went from house to house in one-on-one evangelism daily! *"And daily in the temple, and in every house, they ceased not to teach and preach Jesus Christ" (Acts 5:42).* The Holy Spirit was gushing forth into their lives and they couldn't stop!

When they were persecuted and scattered abroad, they did not stop! Everywhere the believers went, they were spreading the Gospel! *"Therefore, they that were scattered abroad went every where preaching the word" (Acts 8:4). "And they went forth, and preached every where, the Lord working with them, and confirming the word with signs following" (Mark 16:20).*

During this coming Wave of Signs, Wonders and

Miracles, God's supernatural power is going to come gushing forth into the lives of the members of the Body of Christ who are hungry...who are crying out to God and are willing to be used to win souls during these final hours of time. There will be no more "sitting on the sidelines"!

"Those who are unwilling to be soul-winners will miss this wave of the Spirit and will not be part of the true Body of Christ."

As the supernatural power of God is poured out, members of the Body of Christ will have a new authority as they witness on the job to their co-workers, to their families, friends and neighbors. We will be so full of the power and anointing of the Holy Spirit that we will not be able to stop preaching the message of Jesus Christ. Just as people were healed as Peter's shadow fell on them as he walked down the street, everywhere we go there will be manifestations of God's miracle power.

The endtime message we will be preaching will not be a prosperity, "name it-claim it" gospel. We will be **sounding an alarm**! We will be declaring that Jesus Christ is the Son of the living God and that He is the only way of salvation. We will be speaking out against sin, calling men to true repentance and warning of the judgment and wrath of God that is coming upon the earth.

The angel in John's vision proclaimed, *"Fear God, and give glory to him; **for the hour of his judgment is come**: and worship him that made heaven, and earth, and the sea, and the fountains of waters" (Revelation 14:7).*

This is the endtime message we must preach!

Knowing the lateness of the hour and that God's judgments are ready to be poured out upon the wicked, we must not rest or be at ease, we must continually be sounding the alarm...spreading the word...casting out demons...healing the sick...house to house...one on one... snatching souls out of the fire

The World Is Going To Have A Final Endtime Witness Of The Supernatural Power Of God!

As God's people of spiritual destiny, we cannot accomplish the tremendous task God has given us of evangelizing the world in our own limited strength. With all our computer and space-age technology, we cannot do it. We cannot do it using manmade strategies or church programs.

Today there are almost three billion people on the face of this earth who have never once heard the Name of Jesus. Within the Church, there is so little evidence of the miracle power of God in healing the sick, casting out demons and meeting the desperate needs of the world. The Church has failed to produce the evidence…the proof…that Jesus is Who He claims to be.

Something must happen to the Church! The world is going to have a final endtime witness through a manifestation of the supernatural power of God that He is the one true and living God. Just as He manifested Himself in signs and wonders on behalf of Israel and confirmed the Word with signs following in the early Church, He will confirm the Word we speak with signs and wonders!

God has always manifested Himself to His people in signs and wonders. He delivered the Israelites out of Egyptian bondage through signs and wonders which He performed through Moses and Aaron:

He turned the waters into blood (*Exodus 7:17-25*).

He sent a plague of boils upon the magicians and all the Egyptians and their animals, but not on the Israelites (*Exodus 9:9-11*).

He sent a swarm of flies upon the Egyptians but none came upon the Israelites (Exodus 8:21-24).

He sent such darkness that "it could be felt" over the land of Egypt, **yet all the Israelites had light in their dwellings** (*Exodus 10:21-23*).

He rained down fire and hail upon Egypt (*Exodus 9:22-23*).

He sent a plague of locusts that covered the face of the earth (*Exodus 10:12-15*).

He rolled back the waters of the Red Sea and the children of Israel walked across on dry land (*Exodus 14:21-22*).

He supernaturally provided for the children of Israel during their forty years of wanderings in the wilderness…

He provided supernatural guidance…He led them by a pillar of cloud by day and a pillar of fire by night (*Exodus 13:21-22*). The cloud was a covering from the heat of the burning sun (*Psalm 105:39*) and protected them from their enemies (*Exodus 14:19-20*).

He supernaturally fed them daily for forty years by raining manna from heaven (*Exodus 16:35*).

He gave them water to drink by causing water to gush forth out of a rock (*Exodus 17:6*).

He caused their shoes not to wear out (*Deuteronomy 8:4*).

In His covenant relationship with Israel, He continually manifested Himself on their behalf through signs and wonders:

On Mt. Sinai, when He entered into a covenant relationship with Israel, He manifested Himself through signs and wonders...in smoke and fire...and spoke to them out of the fire with an audible voice (*Exodus 3:2-4; Exodus 19:9*).

He supernaturally delivered the Israelites out of the hands of their enemies (*Exodus 23:27; Leviticus 26:7-8*).

He shut the mouth of lions and delivered Daniel out of the lions' den (*Daniel 6:21-22,27*).

He supernaturally protected the three Hebrew children while they were in the fiery furnace and not a hair of their head was singed (*Daniel 3:24-25,28*).

He caused fire to fall from heaven to consume the sacrifice Elijah had prepared, proving that He was the one true God (*I Kings 18:37-39*).

Through Elijah He closed the heavens and it did not rain for a period of three-and-a-half years (*James 5:17*).

He supernaturally fed Elijah by sending a raven to bring him food every day during a time of famine (*I Kings 17:2-6*).

He supernaturally multiplied the widow's cruse of oil and handful of meal and used it to sustain Elijah, the widow woman and her household for two-and-a-half years (*I Kings 17:13-16*).

God manifested Himself to the world through signs, wonders and miracles He worked through Jesus:

Jesus supernaturally provided food for the hungry multitudes by multiplying two small fish and five loaves of bread to feed 5,000 (not counting women and children) (*Matthew 14:17-20*).

He opened blind eyes (*Matthew 11:5*).

He caused the lame to walk (*Matthew 11:5*).

He opened deaf ears (*Matthew 11:5*).

He cleansed the leper and healed all manner of disease (*Matthew 11:5*).

He cast out demons (*Acts 8:7*).

He raised the dead (*Matthew 11:5*).

Through the power and anointing of the Holy Spirit, the believers in the early Church manifested signs, wonders and miracles in the Name of Jesus:

The lame were healed! (*Acts 8:7; Matthew 15:30*).

Demons were cast out! (*Acts 8:7; Acts 5:16*).

The dead were raised! (*Acts 9:40*).

There were mass healings! (*Acts 5:16*).

God supernaturally met all the needs of the believers and there was not one among them that lacked! (*Acts 4:33-34*)

God supernaturally delivered Paul and Silas out of prison. He caused a great earthquake to shake the foundations of the prison until the prison doors were opened and the chains fell off them! (*Acts 16:25-26*).

As Peter was in prison, sleeping between two soldiers, the angel of the Lord appeared, broke the chains off his hands and escorted him out of prison! (*Acts 12:4-11*).

God has not changed!

He is the same all-powerful, supernatural, miracle-working God Who manifests Himself to His people through signs, wonders and miracles! In the decade of the nineties, He is going to pour out His Spirit upon us in an endtime manifestation of His dunamis miracle power that is going to give us the divine capability to fulfill the spiritual destiny of this endtime generation of evangelizing this world before Jesus comes!

The true Body of Christ will be empowered to do the work of the ministry...not just the well-known evangelists, pastors, teachers and ministers from behind the pulpit...but the members of the Body will be going forward with a new authority and a new boldness...one on one, house to house...on the job...at the market place...everywhere they go, until the whole world has been covered with the Gospel.

The Word will be preached by the Body of Christ in a demonstration of God's miracle-working power:

The blind will see!

The lame will walk!

Demons will be cast out!

The Word of God will increase and bring forth a multitude of souls around the world!

God is going to use the Body of Christ...a holy endtime remnant...to manifest His power and bring salvation and deliverance to the world as a final witness before Jesus returns. He is pouring out His Spirit upon us for this specific purpose. Joel prophesied: *"And it shall come to pass, that whosoever shall call on the name of the LORD shall be delivered: for in mount Zion and in Jerusalem shall be deliverance, as the LORD hath said, and **in the remnant** whom the LORD shall call" (Joel 2:32).*

Not only is God going to manifest His signs, wonders and miracles through us, He is going to manifest awesome signs and wonders in the heavens and earth as a final witness to the world to call them to repentance.

God spoke through Joel, *"And I will show wonders in the heavens and in the earth, blood, and fire, and pillars of smoke. The sun shall be turned into darkness, and the moon into blood, before the great and terrible day of the LORD" (Joel 2:30-31).*

The Church will be raptured in a greater demonstration of the miracle power of God than at any other time in the history of mankind!

Just as He delivered Israel out of Pharaoh's hands through a mighty manifestation of signs and wonders, He is going to manifest endtime signs and wonders as He pours out His wrath upon the wicked and gathers His endtime remnant to meet Him in the air.

Just as God turned the waters into blood through Moses and Aaron, He will again turn the waters into blood (*Revelation 16:3*).

Just as He rained down fire and hail upon Egypt, He will rain down fire and hail upon the wicked (*Revelation 8:7; Revelation 16:21*).

Just as He sent darkness upon Egypt but not upon the children of Israel, He will send darkness only upon the Antichrist and his kingdom (*Revelation 16:10-11*).

Just as God sent a plague of boils upon the Egyptians,

He will send a plague of boils upon the Antichrist and all who worship him (*Revelation 16:2*).

Just as He sent a plague of locusts upon Egypt, He will send a plague of locusts upon the wicked (*Revelation 9:1-11*).

There will be a great earthquake, far greater than any this world has ever experienced and beyond man's comprehension (*Revelation 6:12-14; Revelation 16:18-20*).

The sun and the moon will be darkened and the stars will fall from the heavens (*Revelation 6:12-14; Mark 13:24-25; Joel 2:30-31*).

The world is going to have undeniable proof through these endtime signs and wonders that He is the Almighty God...the one true and living God!

In addition to these plagues God is going to pour out upon the wicked, God will manifest signs and wonders through His "two witnesses." For a period of three-and-one-half years, these endtime witnesses, like Moses and Elijah, will have power to call down fire from heaven, shut the heavens from giving rain and power to bring all manner of plagues upon the earth as often as they will! *"And if any man will hurt them, fire proceedeth out of their mouth, and devoureth their enemies; and if any man will hurt them, he must in this manner be killed. These have power to shut heaven, that it rain not in the days of their prophecy: and have power over waters to turn them to blood, and to smite the earth with all plagues, as often as they will"* (*Revelation 11:5-6*).

God will use these endtime witnesses to reveal His power and glory to the world and to call men to repentance. Just as God used the plagues to reveal His miracle power to Pharaoh and Egypt, these endtime witnesses will call for a drought and bring plagues upon the earth as a final warning.

In these closing hours of time, God is going to manifest His power and glory in a greater demonstration of signs, wonders and miracles than at any other time in history. The miracle power of God is going to be released through the Body of Christ in such a great manifestation that multitudes around the world will be saved.

As the supernatural power of God is released and the Body of Christ begins to manifest signs and wonders in the

Name of Jesus, we will face the greatest confrontation of Satan and his demonic forces that the Church has ever known. Satan and his evil principalities will be unleashing their fury and will be doing everything to stop the Church from making inroads into their territory.

One of the five major crises that I shared with you is that we will face a demonic confrontation of gigantic proportions. This confrontation is coming! It is inevitable! As Satan and his demon principalities continue to work through the New Age Movement, the occult and other organizations with an antichrist spirit, to attack the Body of Christ, the Spirit of God is going to give members of the Body a divine capability and a new authority to confront Satan and his demons.

Confrontation is coming. Do not be surprised when it comes, but rather expect it. Put it in your spirit. There are many Christians today who do not like to think about confrontation with Satan and his demons. They are too afraid. They feel unequipped and unable to deal with demon principalities. They would rather take the path of least resistance. In the days to come, there will be no escaping it. You must prepare for it now.

As members of the Body of Christ begin to move out in new power and authority, they will face demonic confrontation on the job, at home, at school, and even in church among fellow Christians. Demon spirits will attack directly through employers, fellow workers, family members, and so-called Christians within the church. You must discern these demon spirits that are working and confront them with the divine capability God is going to manifest within the Church in this coming wave of the Spirit.

In this coming Wave of Signs, Wonders and Miracles, as this spiritual force is released through the Body of Christ, members of the Body will experience a new boldness and fearlessness to confront the enemy. They will not shrink back in fear, but will stand up to the powers of the enemy in direct confrontation.

As the Body of Christ rises up in this new authority to preach the Word in a demonstration of the miracle power of God...on the job...at home...at school...in the marketplace...one on one...house to house...the identity of the demon powers that are working will be revealed. The demon powers and principalities stationed over our cities, over our governments, over our states will be made known to us by the Holy Spirit so that we will be able to confront them directly and break their strongholds.

We Will Have A Divine Capability To Stand Toe To Toe In Direct Confrontation With Satan And His Demons!

When Jesus sent forth His disciples to preach the Gospel, He prepared them for confrontation. He gave them power over demon spirits to cast them out and power to heal all types of sickness.

He warned them of the hatred and persecution they would face. He told them they would be brought before councils, governors and kings for His sake. But He told them not to worry about what they would say because the Spirit of God would speak through them.

Jesus told them that when they were persecuted in one city to go to another one. He commanded them to be fearless. He said: *"**Fear them not therefore**: for there is nothing covered, that shall not be revealed; and hid, that shall not be known. What I tell you in darkness, that speak ye in light: and what ye hear in the ear, that preach ye upon the housetops" (Matthew 10:26).*

He said, *"Fear them not which kill the body but are not able to kill the soul: but rather fear him which is able to destroy both soul and body in hell" (Matthew 10:28).*

Jesus never intended for His disciples to be afraid of confrontation. He did not expect them to run and hide at the first sign of persecution or to stop proclaiming the Gospel. He did not tell them to "water down" or compromise the message for fear of what men might do to them. He told them to shout it from the housetops!

Believers in the early Church did not shrink back in fear. They were not afraid of confrontation. After the apostles were put into prison for preaching the Gospel, God supernaturally delivered them. The angel of the Lord who brought them out of prison told them, *"Go, stand and speak in the temple to the people all the words of this life" (Acts 5:20).* They did not go into hiding or conduct a meeting behind closed doors. The very next morning they fearlessly went into the temple and stood in the midst of the people and taught them about Jesus.

After the great miracle of healing of the lame man at the gate of the temple, Peter stood on Solomon's porch and boldly proclaimed the Gospel of Jesus Christ. When the people saw the miracle...the lame man leaping and praising God...and heard Peter preaching about Jesus, they believed. Think about it! One miracle and five thousand were saved!

Immediately after this manifestation of the miracle power of God, Peter and John faced confrontation! The high priest, Jewish elders and scribes brought them before the council and threatened them so they would not preach or teach in the Name of Jesus. Peter and John were not in the least bit intimidated. They boldly declared, *"For we cannot but speak the things which we have seen and heard" (Acts 4:20).* There was something deep within them that could not be silenced!

When they were released, they did not run and hide somewhere. They did not moan, groan or complain to the other disciples. They did not call a meeting to determine whether or not they should continue to preach or teach openly in the Name of Jesus. They came together in one accord in a prayer meeting. They prayed for boldness and that signs and wonders would be manifested in Jesus' Name.

They cried out to God: *"And now, LORD, behold their threatenings: and grant unto thy servants,* that with all boldness they may speak thy word, By stretching forth thine hand to heal; *and that signs and wonders may be done by the name of thy holy child Jesus" (Acts 4:29-30).*

When they had finished praying, the place where they were meeting was shaken, they were all filled with the Holy Ghost and *"they spake the word of God with boldness" (Acts 4:31).*

This is what must happen to the Body of Christ today to enable us to fulfill endtime spiritual destiny and accomplish the tremendous task before us of evangelizing the world before Jesus comes. We cannot fulfill this task using the same manmade methods and programs we have been using for hundreds of years.

We are only fooling ourselves if we think we will be able to face the demonic confrontation and the coming crises at the current level of our experience in the Church today!

In the decade of the nineties, God does not intend for us to be fearful, weak-kneed or compromising. Regardless of the persecution we will be facing, He does not intend for us to run or hide or be intimidated by the enemy. He does not intend for us to water down the Gospel or stop speaking out against sin. He is going to give us a new boldness to shout the uncompromised Word of God from the housetops!

In this coming wave of Signs, Wonders and Miracles, the Holy Spirit is going to sweep through the Church until the very foundation is shaken by the power of Almighty God. We are going to be filled with a new boldness and fearlessness that is going to enable us to proclaim the Word everywhere we go in a demonstration of the miracle power of God.

As Satan and his demon spirits come against us to stop us, something deep within...a divine capability...a new authority...is going to come gushing forth from deep within us to fortify us. We will not sit back in fear or run from confrontation...we will confront the enemy in the power and authority of the Holy Spirit. There will be something within us that cannot be silenced!

As the Holy Spirit reveals the demon principalities that are attacking our family and loved ones, that are attacking our finances...that have a stronghold over our cities, states and countries...we will not hesitate but will rise up in a new authority to break the enemy's power and take the victory that is ours through Christ.

We will no longer be dealing with Satan and his principalities in broad, vague generalities. Under the unction and power of the Holy Spirit, we will be standing toe to toe with Satan's demons and Satan himself.

In the decade of the nineties, we will not be on the defensive, but will launch a mighty offensive attack against Satan and his demon principalities and take back all that belongs to us as sons of the living God.

In the face of ridicule, hatred and persecution, Christians will become radical in their witnessing. Knowing the lateness of the hour, we will speak under the divine unction and power of the Holy Spirit. And not only will we speak and preach the Word with boldness, God will confirm His Word with signs and wonders!

An outpouring of the Holy Spirit with a manifestation of signs, wonders and miracles greater than anything the world has ever known is coming!

God is going to bring the Body of Christ to a full manifestation of His power and glory as a final endtime witness!

As part of God's people of destiny, He wants YOU to go forward in this decade of the nineties with...

A new authority
A new boldness
A new fearlessness
A divine capability...to fulfill His purposes upon the earth

A new authority...

Jesus said: *"Behold I have given you authority and power to trample on serpents and scorpions, and (physical and mental strength and ability) over all the power that the enemy (possesses), and nothing shall in any way harm you"* *(Luke 10:19, TAB).*

Jesus has given us the power and authority to legally use His Name to heal the sick, cast out devils and to do even greater things than He did.

Jesus has promised: *"And I will do–I Myself will grant– whatever you may ask in My name (presenting all I AM) so that the Father may be glorified and extolled in (through) the Son. (Yes) I will grant–will do for you– whatever you shall ask in My name (presenting all I AM)"* *(John 14:13-14, TAB).*

By faith take hold of these promises and go forward in this decade of destiny with a new authority!

A new boldness...

The early Church knew they needed holy boldness to face the powers of hell and speak the Word without wavering. They met together in one accord and prayed for boldness: *"And when they had prayed, the place where they had gathered together was shaken, and they were all filled with the Holy Spirit, and began to speak the word of God with boldness"* *(Acts 4:31, NAS).*

The Holy Spirit was given to the Body of Christ so that

we will be able to speak the Word of God boldly regardless of the opposition we face. It is one of the evidences of the Holy Spirit. Ask God to fill you with a new boldness to speak the Word in power and to stand up to the power of the enemy and defeat him. Be armed with the **boldness** of the Holy Spirit.

A new fearlessness...

As Jesus sent His disciples out, He commanded them not to fear. He said: *"Fear them not...what I tell you in darkness, that speak ye in light: and what ye hear in the ear, that preach ye upon the housetops" (Matthew 10:26-27).*

He told them: *"And fear not them which kill the body...but rather fear him which is able to destroy both soul and body in hell" (Matthew 10:28).*

God has promised you: *"I will never leave thee, nor forsake thee."*

Therefore we can **boldly** say: *"...The Lord is my helper, and I will not fear what man shall do unto me" (Hebrews 13:6).*

God has commanded you not to fear: *"...Fear not: for I have redeemed thee, I have called thee by thy name; thou art mine. When thou passest through the waters, I will be with thee; and through the rivers, they shall not overflow thee: when thou walkest through the fire, thou shalt not be burned; neither shall the flame kindle upon thee" (Isaiah 43:1-2).*

By faith take hold of God's promises to you and rise up with the offensive weapon of a new fearlessness to stand in direct confrontation with Satan and his demons.

A new capability...

Jesus said: *"But ye shall receive power, after that the Holy Ghost is come upon you: and ye shall be witnesses unto me both in Jerusalem, and in all Judea, and in Samaria, and unto the uttermost part of the earth" (Acts 1:8).*

When the early Church was baptized in the Holy Spirit, they received a divine capability to fulfill the work Christ had given them to do, of evangelizing the world. They did not have the ability within themselves to accomplish this work, but through the Holy Spirit they were given a divine capability to get the job done!

As we enter this decade of the nineties and face this satanic confrontation of gigantic proportions, we must confront and defeat Satan and his demon principalities with a divine capability through the power of the Holy Spirit.

By faith, receive this divine capability and use it as an offensive weapon to defeat the enemy!

Chapter 10

Wave 3: True Unity Through A New Covenant Relationship

You are part of a powerful endtime remnant...God's people of spiritual destiny!

As we enter this last decade of the century, God is raising you up as a manifestation of the power and glory of God to the world. He is preparing and equipping you to go forward in His power and authority to fulfill His purpose and plan in this endtime harvest.

Remember the prophecy God has given us:

A powerful spiritual force is about to be released within the Body of Christ that is going to bring about the greatest demonstration of the power of God the world has ever known!

God has given us the privilege of living in the greatest period of time ever known to man! In this great endtime outpouring before Christ's return, God has shown me...

A Wave Of True Unity Is Coming To The Church!

Following a great sifting that is coming in the Church, producing holiness, there will be a move of the Spirit bringing the Body of Christ together in true unity. Members of the Body of Christ will come together in a new relationship, where we are walking in close covenant relationship with one another...where we will be closer to each other than we are to our own flesh and blood. In this new covenant relationship, we will realize that our true family are those who have been united together in the Spirit.

One of God's major purposes during this great endtime outpouring of the Holy Spirit, is to bring the Body of Christ into full maturity...where we have been molded and conformed into one united Body...where we are a full representation and manifestation of Christ in all His Being!

In this coming Wave of true unity...

The Body of Christ will have a fresh revelation of Christ and all His glory!

We will receive a spiritual breakthrough where we have a clear understanding of what the Body of Christ is.

The Holy Spirit will bind us together in a new bond of God's love.

The Body of Christ will enter into a **new** relationship where we are walking in close covenant relationship with one another.

The Holy Spirit will break down the barriers of selfishness, suspicion, jealousy, competitiveness and pride that are hindering the Body of Christ from functioning together in unity.

Members of the Body of Christ will recognize the sacred relationship and bond as part of the Body of Christ and will give pre-eminence to that relationship above the natural relationship of flesh and blood.

Members of the Body of Christ around the world will recognize they are part of one Body and will make a new, stronger commitment to one another.

Members of the Body of Christ will be molded into one Body where they are functioning together in the unity God intended, which will result in a full manifestation of Christ in all His fullness.

Turn in your Bible to Ephesians, chapter four, and read verses 8-13. Look closely at verse 13. God's purpose for the Body of Christ is... *"Till we all come in the unity of the faith, and of the knowledge of the Son of God, unto a perfect man, unto the measure of the stature of the fulness of Christ" (Ephesians 4:13).*

Now look at this verse in the Amplified version: *"(That it might develop) until we all attain oneness in the faith and in the comprehension of the full and accurate knowledge of the Son of God; that (we might arrive) at really mature manhood—the completeness of personality which is nothing less than the standard height of Christ's own perfection—the measure of the stature of the fullness of the Christ, and the completeness found in Him" (Ephesians 4:13, TAB).*

God's purpose is:

To bring the Body of Christ into unity...oneness in the faith.

To bring us into a full knowledge of Christ.

To bring us to the full stature of Jesus Christ.

Before the Body of Christ can enter into this experience where we are fully mature and functioning at the full capacity God intended for us, we must first come into a new relationship of true unity. We must have a fresh manifestation...a dynamic move of the Holy Spirit that will lift us up from where we are and set us on a higher spiritual plateau.

When we take the mask off and compare the Church with God's original plan and purpose...with what His Church actually is and represents...we are so far off course that it is going to take a supernatural move of the Spirit of God to bring us to the place where God intends for us to be.

Ninety percent of the Church is living a historical, psychosomatic, psychological Christianity. The personal spiritual breakthrough...bringing them out of the natural realm into a living, vibrant relationship with Jesus where the life flow of God is flowing through them to the other members of the Body and to the world...is missing.

In this last decade of the century, there is coming a mighty Wave of the Spirit where Christ will reveal Himself to the Body of Christ as He is in all His glory and majesty! He is going to give us a new and fresh revelation of what the Body of Christ is until we see ourselves through God's eyes as He has planned and purposed for us to be.

Get ready for it...it is coming!

Until we have this fresh revelation...not historical, not doctrinal, not what someone has said in a book...and God gives us a spiritual breakthrough where we can grow up in our understanding and comprehension of Jesus Christ and understand fully who we are and what the Body of Christ is, we will never be able to come together in true unity. Without this move of the Spirit, we will not be able to fulfill the destiny of God...His plan and purpose for the Church when He breathed it into existence. There can be no true relationship until that comes.

In 1987, God gave me a vision in which I saw a mighty

endtime manifestation of the Holy Spirit sweeping through the Church, bringing us into a powerful new dimension of unity.

In this vision, I saw four words that were engulfed and lit up with fire. Those four words were "Unity in the Spirit." The flames of fire I saw in that vision, engulfing the words, are the manifestation of the power of the Holy Spirit.

In the decade of the nineties, a mighty, fiery move of the Holy Spirit is going to sweep throughout the Body of Christ...in North America, Europe, the West Indies, the Philippines, Latin America, Africa, Indonesia, Malaysia... around the world! The Holy Spirit is going to melt our hearts and make us yielded and submissive in the hands of God. By His Spirit working within us, we will be molded into one Body!

When this happens...when we become one, united in the Spirit...get ready! The world is going to see the greatest release of the miracle power of God through the Church it has ever seen. We will be living, walking manifestations of the miracle power of God to the world!

Unity in the Spirit is the key to the release of the power of God within the Body of Christ! It is the key to walking in the fullness of Christ.

This unity that is coming to the Body of Christ is not on the surface. It is not an outward manifestation of various denominations and church organizations uniting together, adhering to certain rules, and coming into agreement on various doctrines and methods of worship. The unity God has planned for us to experience is not a manmade unity...it is a spiritual unity.

Jesus, knowing that He was going to be crucified and that the early Church would face intense persecution after He was gone, prayed for the Church that they would be united into one, just as He and the Father are one.

He prayed: "...*Holy Father, keep through thine own name those whom thou hast given me, that they may be* one, *as we are. That they all may be one; as thou, Father, art in me, and I in thee, that they also may be one in us: that the world may believe that thou hast sent me" (John 17:11,21)*.

It was this unity that enabled the Church to be the powerful force that turned the world upside down! The Church was bound together in such a bond of unity, nothing could stop them...opposition...imprisonment...beatings...death ...nothing!

The Church today is to experience the same unity that Christ has with the Father. Jesus is one with the Father. They are vitally united together by the Spirit. He and the Father are eternally bound together with divine love. Their wills are blended into one. Jesus said, *"My meat is to do the will of him that sent me, and to finish his work" (John 4:34).* He said, *"I and my Father are one" (John 10:30). "The Father is in me, and I in him" (John 10:38).*

The Church is to have this same type of spiritual unity with one another. We are to be vitally united together in a covenant relationship by the same Spirit, possessing the same divine, self-sacrificing love, our minds and wills blended in harmony with the will of God.

When we look at the experience of the Church today, it is difficult to imagine how we could ever experience the same type of unity Christ has with the Father and the same powerful unity the early Church experienced. When the Church was born, it was not divided into a hundred different denominations; believers were united together in the Spirit as one Body.

Now the company of believers was of one heart and soul, and not one of them claimed that anything which he possessed was (exclusively) his own, but everything they had was in common and for the use of all. And with great strength and ability and power, the apostles delivered their testimony to the resurrection of the Lord Jesus, and great grace–loving kindness and favor and goodwill–rested richly upon them all. Nor was there a destitute or needy person among them, for as many as were owners of lands or houses proceeded to sell them, and one by one they brought (gave back) the amount received from the sales And laid it at the feet of the apostles. Then distribution was made according as any one had need" (Acts 4:32-35, TAB).

The members of the Church were of one heart and soul. They were joined together in a powerful covenant relationship with one another wherein they were one in the Spirit.

They were bound together with such a strong bond of love and unselfishness they were willing to sell their houses and lands and give them into a common fund.

In this covenant relationship, they did not selfishly cling to their possessions, but considered them for the common good of all. If a brother or sister had a need, they were ready and willing to give their own possessions to meet their need. If a brother or sister needed clothing, they were willing to give them some of their own clothing. If members of the Body needed food or shelter, they invited them into their own home, fed and housed them until they were able to make it on their own.

When there was a great need among other members of the Body of Christ in other parts of the country, the believers gave unselfishly to meet the needs. During a time of great famine throughout the world, the believers in Antioch gave unselfishly to meet the needs of the members of the Body living in Judea. *"Then the disciples, every man according to his ability, determined to send relief unto the brethren which dwelt in Judea" (Acts 11:29).*

The believers in the churches throughout Macedonia, who themselves were undergoing a great trial of poverty and affliction, disregarded their own great need and gave to meet the needs of the members of the Body in Jerusalem. Paul told the Corinthians: *"For in the midst of an ordeal of severe tribulation, their abundance of joy and their depth of poverty (together) have overflowed in wealth of lavish generosity on their part. For, as I can bear witness, (they gave) according to their ability, yes, and beyond their ability; and (they did it) voluntarily, Begging us most insistently for the favor and the fellowship of contributing in this ministration for (the relief and support of) the saints (in Jerusalem). Nor (was this gift of theirs merely the contribution) that we expected, but first they gave themselves to the Lord and to us (as His agents) by the will of God—that is, entirely disregarding their personal interests, they gave as much as they possibly could, having put themselves at our disposal to be directed by the will of God"* *(II Corinthians 8:2-5, TAB).*

There were no denominational barriers separating them...they were one Body!

Wave 3: True Unity Through A New Covenant Relationship

In contrast, the Body of Christ today is disjointed. We have become separated by denominational barriers and church doctrines. Each denomination is functioning individually as a separate organism with its own set of goals, needs, problems. Each denomination's major concern is its own progress and welfare. Within the denomination itself, there are major conflicts and factions dividing it.

At the local level, we see the same principle repeated. Most local churches today are so totally engrossed in their own efforts, problems and ministering to the needs within their own church body, that they very seldom consider how they are fitting together with other members of the Body of Christ.

Within the churches, smaller groups or factions are operating which are more concerned with doing things their way than they are of keeping unity within the Church. There is envy and strife among members...long-standing feuds...members refusing to talk with one another...rebellion against pastors and church leaders. Pastors are jealous of other pastors...there is criticism and competition between television ministries...and on and on.

The unity God planned for us to experience in this end-time harvest will not be produced by men's futile attempts. It will not be produced by merging denominational forces together. Since the birth of the Church, Christians have had different methodologies, ideas and doctrinal differences.

God doesn't plan to change that. God has not planned for all Christians to act the same...to worship the same way...to look the same...to think the same...to dress the same...to have the same doctrine.

The place where we will be one is not on the surface. It is not in methodology. It is not in ideology or doctrine. The time has come when we must look beyond the idiosyncrasies of our brothers and sisters. It is time for us to get our eyes off methodologies, people's mannerisms and our differences. We must begin to realize there is a place where we can be one without losing our identities.

The place where we can be one is in the Spirit...it is in Jesus. There can be no unity without Him. He is the Head of the Body. As we are joined together in an intimate covenant relationship with Him, we are joined together with one another and we become one in Him.

Paul told the believers in the Corinthian Church: *"For as the body is one, and hath many members, and all the members of that one body, being many, are one body: so also is Christ. For by one Spirit are we all baptized into one body, whether we be Jews or Gentiles, whether we be bond or free; and have been all made to drink into one Spirit"* (I Corinthians 12:12-13).

In God's eyes there aren't hundreds of different churches separated by denominations...there is only one Body!

Paul told the Romans, *"So we, numerous as we are, are one Body in Christ, the Messiah, and individually we are parts one of another, mutually dependent on one another"* (Romans 12:5, TAB).

He told the Ephesians, *"There is one body, and one Spirit, even as ye are called in one hope of your calling; One Lord, one faith, one baptism, One God and Father of all, who is above all, and through all, and in you all"* (Ephesians 4:4-6).

There isn't one Spirit for the Baptists, another Spirit for the Methodists and another for the Pentecostals. We are joined together by the same Spirit.

There can be no real unity with those within the Church claiming to be Christians who are compromising the Word, who are walking after the lusts of the flesh and are part of the apostate church.

In the decade of the nineties, as the Church continues to become polluted through compromise and sin, there will be a separation between the ungodly compromisers and the true saints of God who are walking before Him in holiness. God is calling us to separate ourselves from the apostate church and the world. He is separating the chaff from the wheat.

As this separation takes place, an endtime holy remnant will emerge as the true Body of Christ. This holy remnant will come together in true unity...in the Spirit. They will be bound together in such a bond of love and unselfishness that it will transcend the bonds of flesh and blood.

In this new covenant relationship, members of the Body

of Christ will realize that their true family are those who are united together in the Spirit. We will actually be closer to each other than we are to members of our own family who are unsaved.

A spiritual division is coming where unsaved members of our families will turn against us because of our relationship with Christ and our refusal to compromise with the world. Jesus warned, *"And the brother shall deliver up the brother to death, and the father the child: and the children shall rise up against their parents, and cause them to be put to death" (Matthew 10:21).* In this coming separation, Jesus said, *"A man's foes shall be they of his own household" (Matthew 10:36).*

In the time of intense persecution that I warned you is coming to the Body of Christ before Christ's return, the members of the true Body of Christ will be drawn together in such a strong covenant relationship that they will be willing to unselfishly lay down their own lives for one another.

In the decade of the nineties, as the Body of Christ faces the greatest satanic confrontation we have ever faced, we must come together in true unity. We must break down every barrier that divides us and come into a new relationship with one another where we are one Body...where we are one even as Christ is one with the Father. It is this unity that will release the power of God in our lives and will enable us to be immovable and invincible in the crises we will be facing in the decade of the nineties.

Within the Body of Christ today, there are very few Christians who are walking in covenant relationship with one another. The vast majority of Christians have not had a spiritual breakthrough where they even understand what it means to be in covenant relationship with someone else. Most of the relationships we have within the Body of Christ today are "surface" relationships. Within our local congregations, we do not even know the people we worship together with week after week. We smile, shake hands and see one another from time to time at social functions, but that is the extent of our relationship. We may have a few close friends whom we know on a more intimate basis, but we do not really get to know other members within our own local assemblies.

Most of the time our relationships with other members of the Body are limited to those Christians within the local church where we attend or to those who are members of the same denomination.

The covenant relationship God wants to bring us into in this decade of the nineties is stronger than any natural relationship. He wants us to have the same strong covenant relationship He had when He entered into a blood-covenant relationship with Abraham.

The blood covenant was a form of mutual covenanting between two individuals which was considered the most enduring, most sacred union and held a closer bond than that of being born of the same mother.

In this relationship as "covenant friend" or "blood brother," both individuals were willing to lay down their life in defense of the other...or die in the place of the other. Their enemies became mutual enemies. If a covenant friend was being pursued by an enemy or was at war, the other covenant friend would fight against this enemy with him. Their possessions became their mutual possessions. If they had something their covenant friend desired or needed, there was to be no hesitation...they were obligated to give it freely.

Once this blood covenant was entered into, it was undissolvable. It could not be broken except through death.

This is the type of covenant relationship God entered into with Abraham and has entered into with us.

Just as God has bound Himself to us in a covenant relationship where we are **one** with Him...He is our God and all that He has and is belongs to us...we are to bind ourselves together in a covenant relationship with other members of the Body of Christ, where we are willing to lay down our lives for one another...where their battles become our battles...where we do not selfishly cling to our possessions, but, like the members in the early Church, consider them for the good of all. We are to have a relationship with one another that when our brother or sister has a need, we are willing to share with them what we have.

Wave 3: True Unity Through A New Covenant Relationship

In the decade of the nineties, God wants us to come together in a covenant relationship where members have the same care one for another, when one member suffers, all the members suffer with him or when one member is honored, all the members rejoice with him.

Paul told the Corinthians: *"...But God has combined the members of the body and has given greater honor to the parts that lacked it, so that there should be no division in the body **but that its parts should have equal concern for each other**. If one part suffers, every part suffers with it; if one part is honored, every part rejoices with it"* (I Corinthians 12:24-26, NIV).

He wants us to come into a relationship where we are in actuality bearing one another's burdens...not just talking about it...but actually helping one another to carry their burdens. Paul told the Galatians, *"Bear ye one another's burdens, and so fulfill the law of Christ"* (Galatians 6:2).

God wants us to bear the burdens of members of the Body of Christ in our cities and other parts of the world who are hungry, poor, destitute...who are being persecuted for the sake of the Gospel...who are spiritually hungry for the Word of God and Christian literature.

Before the Body of Christ can come into this strong covenant relationship, it will take a mighty move of the Holy Spirit to break through the barriers we have built that are hindering us from experiencing this unity God has planned for us to have.

It will take a mighty move of the Spirit to break through the selfishness and self-centeredness that has entered into the Body of Christ! We have become so self-centered and focused upon our own needs and the needs of our families that there is no real concern for other members of the Body of Christ in our communities or even in our local congregations who have needs.

It will take a mighty move of the Spirit to rid the Body of Christ of the competitiveness, jealousy, suspicion and pride that separates us and brings division and strife into our churches!

It will take a mighty move of the Spirit to bring us into a bond of God's love for one another that will make us willing

177

to lay down our lives for one another...to lay aside our own desires and give ourselves unselfishly and unreservedly for the sake of other members of the Body of Christ!

Before the Body of Christ can experience true unity and be joined together in this strong covenant relationship, we must first individually have a fresh revelation of what the Body of Christ is.

The Church of Jesus Christ is not a building. It is not a lot of individual churches and denominations who are separated and divided by man-made doctrines and teachings. The Church is not an organization that an individual joins by simply coming before a local church body and agreeing to adhere to its doctrinal teachings and rules.

The Church is the literal Body of Christ. Where the fullness of Christ dwells Christ has been exalted to a position of supreme power and authority over all principalities and powers. In this position He has been made **head** of the Church. Paul told the Ephesians:

And He has put all things under His feet and has appointed Him the universal and supreme Head of the church (a headship exercised throughout the Church), **Which is His body**, *the fullness of Him Who fills all in all—for in that body lives the full measure of Him Who makes everything complete, and Who fills everything everywhere (with Himself)" (Ephesians 1:22-23, TAB).*

We are His Body! We are not a product of man's organization. Members of this sacred Body have been born again by the Spirit of God and have been made part of His living Body!

We have not joined an organization...we have been birthed into His divine Body!

As His Body upon this earth, we are to function together and be a full manifestation of Christ ministering in the same capacity as He did while He was in a physical body upon this earth.

We are not a lot of different organizations or bodies functioning separately...we are one Body. Paul told the Romans, *"So we, numerous as we are, are one Body in Christ, the Messiah, and individually we are parts one of another—mutually dependent on one another" (Romans 12:5, TAB).*

As members of Christ's body, we are joined together with one another in a sacred bond that transcends flesh and blood.

As members of His divine body, we share the same life...His life flows through us, making us one.

We have been baptized by His Spirit into one Body. Paul told the Corinthians: *"And now there are (certainly) many limbs and organs, **but a single body** (I Corinthians 12:20, TAB).* He said, *"Now you (collectively) are Christ's Body and (individually) you are members of it, each part severally and distinct – each with his own place and function" (I Corinthians 12:27, TAB).*

To enter into this covenant relationship, we must recognize this sacred relationship and bond we have as members together of His Body before we will be able to function together in true unity as one Body.

Jesus recognized this spiritual relationship and gave it pre-eminence above man's natural relationship. One day as He was ministering among the people and His disciples, someone came to Him and said, *"Your mother and your brothers are standing outside, seeking to speak to You" (Matthew 12:47, TAB).*

Jesus looked at the man and asked, *"Who is My mother, and who are My brothers?" (Matthew 12:48, TAB).*

Then He stretched out His hand toward His disciples, not just the twelve disciples, but to all those who believed and followed His teachings, and said: *"Here are My mother and My brothers. For whoever does the will of My Father in heaven is My brother and sister and mother!" (Matthew 12:49-50, TAB).*

To walk in true unity, members of the Body of Christ must recognize this sacred bond of the Spirit that transcends man's natural relationships and make a new, stronger commitment to one another.

Recognizing we are joined together as one, we must break down every barrier that would hinder that relationship and the flow of the Spirit through our lives.

We must cry out to God and ask Him to purge and

cleanse our selfishness and pride.

We must take authority over any jealousy, the spirit of competitiveness and suspicion that we have allowed to divide us.

We must look beyond the denominational walls and see one another as members of the same Body...and members one with the other.

A Wave of true unity is coming to the Body of Christ to bring us together and mold us into **one** so that we will stand together as one Body...united by the Spirit...in a full manifestation of Christ to fulfill this endtime destiny.

Chapter 11

Wave 4: Divine Wisdom And Discernment Are Coming

We are entering into the most exciting, challenging period of time the Church has ever known!

It was a great moment in the spiritual destiny of the nation of Israel when Moses led a great victory march of two and one-half million people out of Egypt after 430 years of cruel bondage. Can you imagine that momentous day...the excitement, the shouts of joy, the rejoicing...as the people of God gathered together to make the journey to the land God had promised them as their inheritance?

God had supernaturally delivered them out of the hands of their enemies through a mighty manifestation of signs and wonders and they were marching forward to drive their enemies out and take possession of their land.

The early Church was at a point of great spiritual destiny as it emerged from the Upper Room, full of the power and anointing of the Holy Spirit, to fulfill the divine mandate God had given them of evangelizing the world.

They were being thrust into a time of great uncertainty and upheaval where they were going to face opposition, persecution and death. This small handful of people faced the tremendous challenge of reaching the entire world with the resurrection message of Jesus Christ.

They left the Upper Room, their entire beings literally charged with the power and anointing of the Holy Spirit, fully equipped and prepared to face the onslaught of Satan and fulfill the work God had given them to do!

Today, as the Body of Christ faces this final great moment in spiritual destiny, before Christ's return...where we are going to face the greatest onslaught from Satan the world has ever known, where we are facing the awesome challenge and responsibility of reaching more than two and one-half billion people who have never heard the Name of Jesus...God is sending a mighty endtime outpouring upon us to give us the divine capability and authority to fulfill His plan and purposes in this endtime harvest.

During this endtime outpouring of His Spirit, members of the Body of Christ in every nation upon the face of this earth will be literally charged with the power and anointing of the Holy Spirit and will be used by God as firebrands to spread revival fires throughout their cities, communities and nations. They will speak the Word with such power and anointing that everywhere they go people will be saved, filled with the Holy Ghost and set on fire to work the works of God!

As part of this endtime outpouring, God has shown me He is sending...

A Wave of Wisdom And Discernment Upon The Body Of Christ!

We will experience a manifestation of wisdom, wherein our minds will be anointed and we will know the absolute perfect will of God. It will not be a manifestation of man's natural wisdom and understanding, but an impartation of God's divine wisdom...when words of wisdom are spoken, people will know that this is the voice of God...thus saith the Lord!

In the decade of the nineties, the Body of Christ must have a spiritual breakthrough where our minds have been anointed with God's wisdom and discernment to enable us to face the coming crises and fulfill the plan and purposes He has for us during this endtime harvest. There is no way we can meet the great needs the world is facing today or reach the thousands of souls who are dying without God, depending upon our own wisdom.

One of the major reasons the Church has not been able to do in 2,000 years what the early Church accomplished in 200 years, is because we have been functioning according to man's natural wisdom and understanding instead of looking to and depending upon God to give us His wisdom.

God's plan and purpose from the very beginning has been to reveal His wisdom through the Church. Paul told the Ephesians: *"Although I am less than the least of all God's people, this grace was given me: to preach to the Gentiles the unsearchable riches of Christ, and to make plain to everyone the administration of this mystery, which for ages past was kept hidden in God, who created all things.* **His intent was that now, through the Church, the manifold wisdom of God should be made known to the rulers and authorities in the heavenly realms according to his eternal purpose which he accomplished in Christ Jesus our Lord"** *(Ephesians 3:8-11, NIV).*

Within the heart and mind of God, He planned and purposed to send Christ to the world to redeem and restore man to Himself and to join Jews and Gentiles together in one Body as joint heirs in the Kingdom of God. He planned that Christ would dwell within man by His Spirit, reproducing His life within them.

This plan was hidden within God throughout the ages. Not even the heavenly principalities and powers knew God's plan concerning what Paul referred to as "the mystery of Christ." God chose to reveal His mind...His wisdom...His eternal purposes that were kept within His heart and mind through His Church. Paul said, *"His intent was that now, through the church, the manifold wisdom of God should be made known to the rulers and authorities in the heavenly realms" (Ephesians 3:10, NIV).*

God's purpose today is that through Christ not only will we be able to have His wisdom operating in our lives, but that it be manifested to the world and the heavenly principalities!

God is not withholding His wisdom from us. His plan is that our hearts and minds be anointed by His Spirit so that we will have His wisdom and knowledge in both the spiritual and natural realms. It is His will that you be filled with His wisdom and spiritual discernment.

Paul told the Colossians: *"For this reason we also, from the day we heard of it, have not ceased to pray and make (special) request for you, (asking)* **that you may be filled with the full (deep and clear) knowledge of His will in all spiri-**

tual wisdom (that is, in comprehensive insight into the ways and purposes of God) and in understanding and discernment of spiritual things" (Colossians 1:9, TAB).

His purpose for giving us this wisdom and discernment is: *"...that you may live a life worthy of the Lord and may please him in every way: bearing fruit in every good work, growing in the knowledge of God, being strengthened with all power according to his glorious might so that you may have great endurance and patience..." (Colossians 1:10-11, NIV).*

God has planned for us to have His wisdom and spiritual discernment:

So we will be able to know His will, His plan and purposes.

So we will be able to fulfill His will and be fruitful in every good work.

So we will grow in knowledge of Him.

So we will be strengthened with all power and have endurance!

Paul prayed for the Ephesians: *"That the God of our Lord Jesus Christ, the Father of glory, may give unto you the spirit of wisdom and revelation in the knowledge of him: The eyes of your understanding being enlightened; that ye may know what is the hope of his calling, and what the riches of the glory of his inheritance in the saints, And what is the exceeding greatness of his power..." (Ephesians 1:17-19).*

Paul prayed that God would give to the believers in the Ephesian churches a spirit of wisdom and revelation in the knowledge of Christ, so that their minds would be anointed to know and understand God's plan and purposes...the hope of His calling...the riches of the glory of His inheritance in the saints...the exceeding greatness of His power!

With our natural minds we cannot possibly know God or His will. Our natural or "carnal" minds cannot perceive the things of God. Paul said, *"The natural man receiveth not the things of the Spirit of God: for they are foolishness unto him: neither can he know them, because they are spiritually discerned (I Corinthians 2:14).*

When God created man, he was created in God's own

image. Adam's mind was perfectly whole in every way. He was filled with God's wisdom and understanding. His mind was in perfect harmony with God's will.

As a result of man's fall, man lost this ability. He was not only unable to know or comprehend God, his mind was alienated and opposed to God. *"...the sinful mind is hostile to God. It does not submit to God's law, nor can it do so" (Romans 8:7, NIV).*

Through Christ, that ability has been restored and we can have His mind...where God's wisdom is imparted to us by His Spirit. Paul told the Corinthians, *"But we have the mind of Christ, the Messiah, and do hold the thoughts (feelings and purposes) of His heart" (I Corinthians 2:16, TAB).*

God does not want us to live our lives according to our limited natural minds. He has made it possible for us to be filled with His wisdom and spiritual discernment. He does not want us to depend upon our natural wisdom on our jobs, in providing for our families, in making major decisions or any other aspect of our natural lives. Neither does He want us to try to fulfill His will and do the work of the ministry in our own limited natural understanding.

The believers and apostles in the early Church did not try to fulfill the work of the ministry and evangelize the world in the strength and ability of their own wisdom. Paul said, *"And my speech and my preaching was not with enticing words of **man's wisdom**, but in demonstration of the Spirit and of power: That your faith should not stand in the **wisdom of men, but in the power of God**" (I Corinthians 2:4-5).*

Paul was not relying upon his natural wisdom. He said, "I'm not coming to you with man's wisdom, preaching and teaching what man has revealed. I'm coming to you in a demonstration of the Spirit and power." He was preaching and teaching revelation knowledge...God's wisdom that had been revealed to him by the Spirit!

He told them: *"Howbeit we speak wisdom among them that are perfect: yet not the wisdom of this world, nor of the princes of this world, that come to nought: But we speak the **wisdom of God** in a mystery, even the hidden wisdom, which God ordained before the world unto our glory" (I Corinthians 2:6-7).*

185

Paul was saying, "I'm not speaking man's wisdom. I'm speaking God's wisdom!"

Before He formed the world, God planned for us to have His wisdom manifested through us. He ordained from the beginning to reveal His wisdom and make it known through us for our glory. We are to speak, preach and teach according to God's wisdom, not our own.

The wisdom that comes from God is not a product of the natural mind. It does not come as a result of research or study. Neither is it a product of this world. It does not come from the outstanding scientists or leading intellects of our day. Paul said, *"For the wisdom of this world is foolishness with God" (I Corinthians 3:19)*. He told the Corinthians that he did not "speak the wisdom of the world, nor of the princes of this world, **that come to nought**." The wisdom Paul had received and taught was not a worldly wisdom that came from the leaders or rulers of the age, who are brought to nothing and pass away. He had received supernatural wisdom and revelation which had been imparted to him from God.

The wisdom from God is supernatural. It comes from the supreme mind of God and reveals His will, His thoughts and His purposes. The apostle James said, *"But the wisdom from above is first pure, then peaceable, gentle, reasonable, full of mercy and good fruits, unwavering, without hypocrisy" (James 3:17, NAS)*.

Paul exclaimed: *"O the depth of the riches and wisdom and knowledge of God! How unfathomable (inscrutable, unsearchable) are His judgments–His decisions! And how untraceable (mysterious, undiscoverable) are His ways–His methods, His paths (Romans 11:33, TAB)*.

God has not only chosen to reveal the unsearchable depths of His divine wisdom to us, but to impart it to us...to anoint our minds with it.

Paul said: *"For who has known or understood the mind (the counsels and purposes) of the Lord so as to guide and instruct (Him) and give Him knowledge?* **But we have the mind of Christ, the Messiah, and do hold the thoughts (feelings and purposes) of His heart"** *(I Corinthians 2:16, TAB)*.

God has ordained that we live our lives according to His

divine wisdom. He wants us to walk in His divine wisdom. By His Spirit He has revealed His divine counsels, His will, thoughts and purposes to us so that we may know and partake of all the things He has prepared for us.

Paul told the Corinthians: *"But we speak the wisdom of God in a mystery, even the hidden wisdom, which God ordained before the world unto our glory: Which none of the princes of this world knew: for had they known it, they would not have crucified the Lord of glory. But as it is written, Eye hath not seen, nor ear heard, neither have entered into the heart of man, the things which God hath prepared for them that love him.* **But God has revealed them unto us by his Spirit**; *for the Spirit searcheth all things, yea, the deep things of God"* (I Corinthians 2:7-10).

God has revealed to us by His Spirit His wisdom...His plan, purpose and will toward us. What *"Eye hath not seen, nor ear heard,"* concerning the deep things of God, He has revealed to us. He has revealed the unsearchable riches that we have in Christ. He has revealed the secret counsels and wisdom of God. Paul said the Spirit searches all the deep things of God and reveals them to us.

Paul said: *"For who among men knows the thoughts of a man except the spirit of the man, which is in him? Even so the thoughts of God no one knows except the Spirit of God. Now we have received, not the spirit of the world, but the Spirit who is from God,* **that we might know** *the things freely given to us by God"* (I Corinthians 2:11-12, NAS).

The Spirit searches the depths of the counsels, thoughts, purposes and will of God. The same Spirit that is in God...that is one with God...is in us. God has placed His Spirit within us so we can know and walk in His divine wisdom!

God's purpose for our lives today is that we be *"filled with the knowledge of His will in all wisdom and spiritual understanding!" (Colossians 1:9).*

James said, *"But if any of you lacks wisdom, let him ask of God, who gives to all men generously and without reproach, and it will be given to him" (James 1:5, NAS).*

In the decade of the nineties, a Wave of Wisdom and

Discernment is coming to the Body of Christ and we are going to walk in God's wisdom.

The Spirit of God will anoint our minds and impart to us God's wisdom to know His perfect will. In the situations and circumstances we face, we will know and speak forth words of wisdom that are direct from the throne of God!

To fulfill the great spiritual destiny that is before us in these final days before Christ's return, the Body of Christ must have this divine impartation of God's wisdom. There is no way we are going to be able to fulfill the divine mandate He has given us of evangelizing the world in our own limited natural wisdom and understanding.

Think about all that is coming in the five major crises I have shared with you, which God has already revealed to us:

Crisis 1. A Crisis of Change...
Worldwide economic change
Major changes within the traditional structure of the Church
Increased hatred and persecution of the Body of Christ
Increase of natural disasters

Crisis 2. A Crisis of the Family...
Spiritual division
Increase of domestic violence, incest and child abuse
An ever-increasing breakdown of moral standards
Continued breakdown of family unit through humanism and New Age teachings

Crisis 3. A Crisis of the Church...
Separation of the Body of Christ from uncommitted, compromising Christians
Restoration of five-fold ministry to the Church

Crisis 4. A Major Worldwide Financial Crisis...

Crisis 5. A Satanic Confrontation of Gigantic Proportions
Increase in occultic and demonic activity
Increase of sin...violence...crime
A wave of satanic deception
Greatest confrontation and assault from Satan and his principalities man has ever known or experienced!

There is no way that we can face these crises and the challenges that are before us in our own wisdom. We must have a divine impartation of God's wisdom!

In the decade of the nineties, as the Body of Christ goes forth to preach the Word, witness, heal the sick and do the works of God...

There will be a divine impartation of God's wisdom to know God's perfect will.

There will be a divine impartation of God's wisdom to ministers and evangelists, revealing to them what cities to go to, to conduct meetings.

There will be a divine impartation of God's divine wisdom, giving them new God-given ideas, methodologies and strategies, enabling them to be more effective in their ministries.

There will be a divine impartation of God's wisdom in the natural realm, where the minds of God's people will be anointed to know what to do in the problems they are facing...on the job, at home, in their finances.

In the decade of the nineties, as we face the worldwide economic upheaval, God will anoint the minds of His people with His wisdom so they will be able to know how to cope with the problems they will be facing in their finances.

In the decade of the nineties, as we face this satanic confrontation...where we will face direct confrontation with Satan and his demons...the Spirit of God will give us a spirit of discernment to know the names of the demons that are attacking us so we can take authority over them and drive them out.

In the coming wave of deception, we will have an impartation of God's wisdom so we will be able to discern the false doctrines and lies of Satan.

In the decade of the nineties, as we face intense persecution for the sake of the Gospel, God will anoint our minds with His wisdom. The Spirit of God within us will quicken the Word to our minds and we will speak it forth under the unction and power of the Holy Spirit.

Jesus said that this time of persecution will be an opportunity for us to bear witness. He said: *"This will be a time (an opportunity) for you to bear testimony. Resolve and settle it in your minds, not to meditate and prepare before- hand how you are to make your defense and how you will answer.* **For I (Myself) will give you a mouth and such utter-**

ance and wisdom as all of your foes combined will be unable to stand against or refute" (*Luke 21:13-15, TAB*).

As you enter this decade and take your position as one of God's people of destiny and make a 100 percent commitment to Him to fulfill His will, this is Christ's promise to you: He will give you divine wisdom that none of your enemies will be able to stand against!

Prepare yourself now for this coming Wave of Wisdom and Discernment. In the daily circumstances you face, don't rely upon your own wisdom...look to God for His wisdom.

In the family or financial problems you are facing, don't try to work them out according to your own wisdom...ask God to anoint your mind and give you His wisdom so that you will know His perfect will and will know what action you should take.

Fill your heart and mind with the Word of God. Paul said: "Let the word of Christ dwell in you richly **in all wisdom**" (Colossians 3:16). Christ and His Word are inseparable. In Him is **all** wisdom. Paul told the Colossians: *"In Him all the treasures of (divine) wisdom, (of comprehensive insight into the ways and purposes of God), and (all the riches of spiritual) knowledge and enlightenment are stored up and lie hidden" (Colossians 2:3, TAB).*

He told the Corinthians: *"But of him are ye in Christ Jesus, who of God is made unto us* wisdom, *and righteousness, and sanctification, and redemption" (I Corinthians 1:30).*

Meditate upon the Word and stay in constant communion with Christ. Walk in covenant relationship with Him where you are one with Him. Then, as you face problems, challenges and circumstances in your life, ask God to anoint your mind and give you His divine wisdom.

It is time to enter into a new spiritual dimension where you are walking in God's divine wisdom in every area of your life.

Chapter 12

Wave 5: Restitution And Restoration For The Church!

We have entered into the decade of the nineties...the last decade of the twentieth century! God has been positioning and preparing the Body for this period of spiritual destiny, where we are going to experience the greatest manifestation and outpouring of the Spirit of God the world has ever known...where there is a full manifestation of His power flowing through the true Body of Christ!

Have you taken your position as part of God's people of destiny? As I have been sharing with you the revelation God has given me concerning the coming Five Major Crises and Five Major Waves of the Spirit, have you been preparing yourself and acting on what God has been quickening to your spirit?

It is not enough for you to know the crises we will face and how the Spirit of God will be moving. To take your position, you must be willing to move into a new spiritual dimension, where you are not only **hearing** what the Spirit of God is saying, but where you are 100 percent sold out, committed to God and doing the work He has called us to do. These final hours of time before Christ's coming, you must be willing to get off the sidelines, shake yourself from all complacency and by faith launch out into a new territory. You must be willing to get out of the comfortable pew and into the "heat" of battle.

As I share with you another major Wave of the Spirit God has shown me that is coming in the decade of the nineties, take your position as part of God's people of spiritual destiny by acting upon what God reveals to you. Don't allow Satan to hinder you from being part of this great end-time move of God.

A New Wave Of Restitution And Restoration Is Coming! This Wave of Restoration will enable us to experience total restoration in every aspect of our beings...spirit... soul...body. We will rise up in a new authority to take back all that Satan has stolen from us!

In the decade of the nineties, we will see a powerful wave of the Spirit flow through the Body of Christ, bringing us into a new spiritual dimension of restoration.

Satan is a liar and a thief! For thousands of years he has been lying and robbing God's people of the blessings God has provided for us through Christ. Through our lack of knowledge, we have been living far below our rights and privileges. Through the great victory Christ won for us through His life, death and resurrection, we have already been fully restored with full rights and privileges as sons of God and joint heirs of the kingdom of God! Yet through our lack of **revelation knowledge**, we have allowed Satan to rob us of our spiritual inheritance.

In these final days before Christ's return, a wave of the Holy Spirit is coming to bring total restoration to the Body of Christ, where we have reclaimed all the things that rightfully belong to us. We are going to come to a point of spiritual maturity where we have grown to the full stature of Jesus Christ...where, Christ, in all His fullness is manifested in us.

Following the day of Pentecost, Peter preached a sermon to the multitude who had gathered following the healing of the lame man. In that sermon he called the people to repentance and referred to a coming time of restoration. He said: *"Repent therefore and return, that your sins may be wiped away, in order that times of refreshing may come from the presence of the Lord; and that He may send Jesus, the Christ appointed for you,* **whom heaven must receive until the period of restoration of all things about which God spoke by the mouth of His holy prophets from ancient time**" (*Acts 3:19-20, NAS*).

Peter said that Christ must remain in heaven *"until the times of restitution of all things, which God hath spoken by the mouth of all his holy prophets since the world began"* (*Acts 3:21*).

The Greek word for "restoration" is "apokatastasis,"

which means "to set in order; to bring back into former position; to bring to a healthy state." Restoration also includes "regeneration," which involves the creation of new things. Regeneration means "to be restored to a better, higher or more worthy state; to produce anew."

From the beginning of time God planned to restore...to bring man and the whole universe back into a perfect state of total wholeness and perfect harmony with Him. Since the world began, through His prophets He promised this restoration. The "times of restitution" Peter referred to is a period of restoration **before Christ's coming** when the divine plan and purposes of God will be fully accomplished in bringing man and the universe back into harmony with Him.

The apostle Paul wrote to the Ephesians about this time of restoration. He said: *"Having made known unto us the mystery of his will, according to his good pleasure which he hath purposed in himself: **That in the dispensation of the fulness of times** he might gather together in one all things in Christ, both which are in heaven, and which are on earth: even in him" (Ephesians 1:9-10).*

Paul said in the fullness of times God has planned to "bring all things in heaven and in earth together"...head them up and consummate them in Christ. We are living in the fullness of time when God will restore...set in order and bring all things together into harmony with Him!

Before the foundation of the earth, God developed a plan whereby we would be restored to a state of total wholeness and be reconciled to Him through Christ. Throughout the ages He has been working to fulfill this plan. Some things have been restored, while others are in the process of being restored. Now, in these final days before Christ's return, all the promises He has made concerning restoration are going to be consummated and brought to fulfillment.

During this coming Wave of Restoration, the Body of Christ will be restored and brought to a new position where we have reached the perfection...full maturity that is possible in Christ. In this position we will experience a total wholeness...where Christ in all His fullness will be manifested in us.

As part of God's plan of restoration, He planned, even before He formed the earth, that we would be changed and conformed into the image of Christ. Paul told the Romans: *"And we know that all things work together for good to them that love God, to them who are the called **according to his purpose**. Now, look, closely at God's purpose: For whom he did foreknow, he also did predestinate to be **conformed to the image of his Son**, that he might be the firstborn among many brethren" (Romans 8:28-29).*

The Greek word for "conformed" is "summorphos," which means "having the same form as another; conformed to."

God's plan and purpose for us is not that we should simply bear a likeness or resemblance to Christ, but that we be changed and conformed into the same image as Christ! Paul told the Galatians, *"My little children, of whom I travail in birth again until **Christ be formed in you**" (Galatians 4:19).* It is God's purpose that the fullness of Christ in all His being be fully formed within us reproducing His exact image.

Paul was not referring to a physical transformation of our bodies. That will take place at Christ's coming. He was referring to an inner transformation within us, where our carnal nature is dead and Christ in all His fullness is being reproduced within us. We are now being constantly transformed into the same image of Christ. Paul told the Corinthians *"But we all, with open face beholding as in a glass the glory of the Lord, are **changed into the same image** from glory to glory, even as by the Spirit of the Lord" (II Corinthians 3:18).*

The word "changed" in this verse is translated from the Greek word, "metamorphos," which means "transformed; transfigure; to change into another form." It is the same word that is used to describe the transformation that took place when Christ was "transfigured" before His disciples (Matthew 17:2). At His transfiguration, Christ was visibly changed. The glory...Doxa...of God...radiated through His face and entire being.

God's plan and purpose for us is that we be continually transformed by His Spirit working within us until we are changed into the same image of Christ. The word "image" is translated from the Greek word "eikon," which involves the two concepts of representation and manifestation. To be changed into the same image of Christ means more than a mere likeness or resemblance...it is an actual representation and manifestation of all that Christ is.

From the very beginning, God planned for man to be made in His own image...as a representation of Who He was. He said: *"...Let us make man **in our image, after our likeness**: and let them have dominion over the fish of the sea, and over the fowl of the air, and over the cattle, and over all the earth, and over every creeping thing that creepeth upon the earth" (Genesis 1:26).*

When God created Adam and Eve and placed them in the Garden of Eden, He created them in His own image. They were made as a representation of God and His glory. *"So God created man in his own image, in the image of God created he him; male and female created He them" (Genesis 1:27).*

Think about it. The all-powerful, Almighty God created man in His own image. He exalted man and placed him in a position of power, authority and dominion over the earth. He created man to rule the earth. He told them to subdue and take dominion of the earth. He said: *"...Be fruitful, and multiply, and replenish the earth, and subdue it: and have dominion over the fish of the sea, and over the fowl of the air, and over every living thing that moveth upon the earth" (Genesis 1:28).*

Man, who was created in God's image, was pure... holy...without sin. His spirit, soul and body were in perfect harmony with God. He was filled with the knowledge and wisdom of God. He possessed the ability to rule over every aspect of his mind...his thoughts...imaginations...emotions...will. He was full of God's love and enjoyed intimate communion and fellowship with God. God came down and walked and talked with them.

Man was a perfect creation of God. He was perfectly whole in every way...spirit, soul and body. He had no physical defects, disabilities or limitations. There was no pain, sickness or death. God intended for man to live forever. When Adam and Eve yielded their wills to Satan and rebelled against God, they ceased to be a representation of the glorious image of God.

Man lost his sinless perfection!

Man lost his intimate fellowship and communion with God!

Man lost his spiritual position where his spirit, soul and body were in perfect harmony with the will of God!

Man lost his ability to rule over his mind...to control his thoughts, imagination, emotions and will!

Man lost his position of power and authority!

The ground was cursed!

Sin, sickness and death came upon the earth!

From his exalted position of power, authority and dominion, as a representation of God, man became a slave. He no longer had the ability to rule over his spirit, he was ruled over by Satan. Satan gained power over man's mind, thoughts, imaginations and will. Man's relationship with God was severed. In his sinful condition, he no longer had the freedom or privilege of coming into God's Presence.

Christ Has Restored To Man All That Adam Lost And More!

One of the lies Satan has been using to keep the Body of Christ from taking possession of our spiritual inheritance and all that God has made possible for us through Christ is the lie that when Adam and Eve disobeyed God and yielded their wills to him, Satan gained control and dominion over this earth. **God did not lose control over the earth to Satan. He always has been...He is now...He always will be in control!**

Satan is a liar! The earth does not belong to him! He does not have power and dominion over this earth! God did not turn the earth over to him *"The earth is the LORD'S, and the fullness thereof; the world, and they that dwell therein" (Psalm 24:1).* God, the creator of all living things, did not lose control over the earth to Satan.

What Satan did gain control and dominion over was the spirits of Adam and Eve. He ruled over them. As the "prince of this world," Satan rules over the darkness...the evil powers and principalities of this world and all those who are under his control. He does not have power, authority and dominion over this earth! He does not have power and authority over God's people!

Wave 5: Restitution and Restoration For The Church!

Through Christ, God has restored to man all that Adam lost and more! He has restored us to total wholeness that is possible in Christ.

In accordance with His divine plan of restoration, God sent Jesus to redeem and restore man to an even greater position of power and authority as His very own sons.

"But when the fulness of the time was come, God sent forth his Son, made of a woman, made under the law, To redeem them that were under the law, that we might receive the adoption of sons. And because ye are sons, God hath sent forth the Spirit of his Son into your hearts, crying, Abba, Father. Wherefore thou art no more a servant, but a son; and if a son, then an heir of God through Christ" *(Galatians 4:4-7).*

Christ is the "express image" of God. He was a visible representation and manifestation of God to the world. Paul told the Hebrews Christ was *"the brightness of his glory, and the express image of his person"* *(Hebrews 1:3).*

He told the Colossians that God has delivered us: *"...from the power of darkness, and hath translated us into the kingdom of his dear Son: In whom we have redemption through his blood, even the forgiveness of sins: Who is the **image of the invisible God**, the firstborn of every creature"* *(Colossians 1:13-15).*

Christ is the express image of God. He is a full manifestation of the power and glory of God. Paul told the Colossians, *"For it pleased the Father that in him should all fulness dwell"* *(Colossians 1:19).* He said: *"For in him dwelleth all the fulness of the godhead bodily. And ye are **complete** in him, which is the head of all principality and power"* *(Colossians 2:9-10).*

The Greek word for "fulness" in these verses is "pleroma," which refers to God, in the completeness of His being.

As the express image of God, the fullness of the Godhead...all the divine attributes of God...His infinite wisdom...His love...His righteousness...His faithfulness...His power...reside in Christ.

Jesus, Who was and is the express image...the visible representation and manifestation of God...defeated Satan!

He destroyed the works of Satan!

197

He broke the power of sin, sickness and death!

He restored and elevated man to an even greater position than Adam!

He has removed our sins from us and has restored us into close fellowship and communion with God and elevated us to the position of joint heirs with Him!

He has restored our ability to rule over our spirits and minds...control our thoughts, imaginations and wills!

He has restored us to total wholeness...where it is possible for every aspect of our beings...spirits, souls and bodies...to be brought into complete harmony with the will of God!

He has restored us to a position of power, authority and dominion over the earth!

The Body of Christ today is living far below all that God has already provided for us to have. We have listened to Satan's lies too long!

Instead of taking our position of power and authority over the earth, we have listened to Satan's lie that he is in control and have allowed him to have dominion.

Instead of bringing our minds...thoughts...imaginations and wills into submission and obedience to God and His word, we have listened to Satan's lie that it is not possible.

Instead of taking the healing that belongs to us, we have allowed Satan to bring sickness and disease upon us.

Instead of taking our position as restored sons of God and taking possession of our spiritual inheritance as sons of God and joint-heirs of the Kingdom of God, we have settled...

This is a day of revelation...of restoration!

It is time for the Body of Christ to take back all the things Satan has stolen from us!

It is time for us to take the position Christ has restored us to!

God's plan and purpose for us today is that just as Christ was the express image of God...a visible representation and manifestation of Him, we are to be the same image...a visible representation and manifestation...of Christ in the fullness of His being!

We have not been restored to the stature of Adam, but to the stature of the second Adam, Jesus Christ. We are to bear

His image. We are not to merely resemble Christ, but we are to be changed into His same image within our inner man, where we are an accurate representation and manifestation of Him...where His life is reproduced in us...where we are manifesting His love...His righteousness...His wisdom...His power and glory to the world.

You may look at your own level of experience and wonder how it could ever be possible for you to be changed into the same image of Christ. Regardless of your current level of experience or of the majority of Christians today, it does not nullify or make void the Word of God.

God's intention for the Church is that we be perfected ...brought to full maturity...to where we have reached the full stature of Jesus Christ. Paul told the Ephesians: *"His intention was the perfecting and the full equipping of the saints (His consecrated people), (that they should do) the work of ministering toward building up Christ's body (the church), (That it might develop) until we all attain oneness in the faith and in the comprehension of the full and accurate knowledge of the Son of God; that (we might arrive) at really mature manhood—the completeness of personality which is nothing less than the standard height of Christ's own perfection—the measure of the stature of the fullness of the Christ, and the completeness found in Him"* (Ephesians 4:12-13, TAB).

The "fulness" of Christ in these verses refers to Christ in the completeness of His being. Paul said, *"For in him dwelleth all the fulness of the godhead bodily. And ye are complete in him, which is the head of all principality and power"* (Colossians 2:9-10).

You and I are to be filled with the fullness of Christ! We are to have His life...His righteousness...His love...His will...His wisdom...His mind...His power...manifested in us.

Paul, referring to Christ, said: *"And He has put all things under His feet and has appointed Him the universal and supreme Head of the church (a headship exercised throughout the church) Which is His body, the fulness of Him Who fills all in all—for in that body lives the full measure of Him Who makes everything complete, and Who fills everything everywhere (with Himself)"* (Ephesians 1:22-23, TAB).

We are to be filled with the full measure of Christ!

In this coming Wave of Restoration, the Spirit of God is going to restore the Body of Christ and bring us to full spiritual maturity where Christ in all His fullness is manifested through us. By His Spirit working within us, He has been changing us...conforming us...molding us...into the same image of Christ. Paul said we are being "changed into the same image from glory to glory, even **as by the Spirit of the Lord**." It is the Spirit of the Lord working within us that is changing us into the same image of Christ.

We have not reached this position of spiritual maturity because we have limited God. In our natural minds we have not been able to conceive how it could be possible for us to be changed into Christ's image. Our God is *"able to do exceeding abundantly above all that we ask or think, according to the power that worketh in us" (Ephesians 3:20)*. It is not us...it is the power of Almighty God within us that is going to do the work!

When we were born again, God placed His Spirit within us and the life of Christ was birthed within us. It was not something we did, it was the work of the Spirit. All we did was come to God and surrender our wills to Him. He performed the work within us by His Spirit.

Paul told the Corinthians: *"But we have this treasure in earthen vessels, that the excellency of the power may be of God, and not of us" (II Corinthians 4:7)*.

God has placed within you the very life of Christ. In this time of restoration, He will, by His Spirit working within you, bring you to full spiritual maturity where you have been changed into the same image of Christ...as a representation and manifestation of all that Christ is.

During this Wave of Restoration that is coming in the decade of the nineties, God wants us to **rise up** in faith and take hold of this position He has restored us to. We must yield ourselves to God and allow His Spirit to work within us to purge and cleanse us until we are molded into Christ's image.

Here are four things God wants to restore in our lives:

1. God wants us to take our rightful position of power, authority and dominion!

2. He wants us to take hold of His promises and take back all that Satan has stolen from us!

3. He wants us to walk in His strength and power!

4. He wants us to experience His supernatural provision in our lives, where all our needs are met!

The Body Of Christ Will Experience Total Restoration

A powerful Wave of Restitution and Restoration is coming! In this decade of spiritual destiny, during this great endtime outpouring, the Holy Spirit is going to be released within the Body of Christ, bringing restoration in every aspect of our lives.

Here are five specific areas of our lives where God wants to manifest His endtime wave of restoration:

1. Restoration of our position of power and authority!

2. Restoration in our minds...thoughts, imaginations, wills!

3. Restoration in our families!

4. Restoration in our health!

5. Restoration in our finances!

In this coming Wave of Restoration, we will see the restoration of the nation of Israel. God will not forget or break His covenant with Abraham. All the promises He has made concerning the restoration of Israel will be fulfilled. Right before our eyes we have already seen many of these prophecies fulfilled.

The prophecies concerning the restoration of Israel are parallel with the restoration that is coming to the Body of Christ. We are God's spiritual Israel. As we look at God's promises of restoration to Israel, you will see more clearly the restoration that is coming to the Body of Christ.

As part of God's plan of restoration, He bound Himself together in a covenant with Abraham. He promised *"And I will make of thee a great nation, and I will bless thee, and make thy name great; and thou shalt be a blessing: And I will bless them that bless thee, and curse him that curseth thee: and in thee shall all families of the earth be blessed"* *(Genesis 12:2-3).*

Four hundred and thirty years after this covenant was made between God and Abraham, the Law was given to Moses as a temporary means of reconciling and restoring man to God.

With the Law, God gave the Israelites a choice...to obey and be blessed, or to disobey and be cursed.

The Israelites turned their backs on God and through their disobedience brought the curses God had warned them about (*Deuteronomy 28:15-68*).

God hid His face from Israel. (*Isaiah 54:7-8*)

Their land became barren and desolate. (*Deuteronomy 28:38-40,42; Joel 1:4,10-11*)

Sickness and disease came upon them. (*Deuteronomy 28:21,27,35,59-61*)

They suffered adversity and want "of all things." (*Deuteronomy 28:48*)

They were taken captive by their enemies. (*Deuteronomy 28:50-52; Joel 1:6*)

They were scattered to the corners of the earth. (*Deuteronomy 28:64*)

They were smitten with spiritual blindness. (*Deuteronomy 28:28,29*)

All these things came upon Israel as a result of their disobedience.

Through all their backslidings, rebellion and hardening of their hearts toward God, He did not forsake Israel. He was bound to them by His covenant and His great love for them. God promised Israel: *"And yet for all that, when they be in the land of their enemies, I will not cast them away, neither will I abhor them, to destroy them utterly, and to break my covenant with them: for I am the LORD their God. But I will for their sakes remember the covenant of their ancestors, whom I brought forth out of the land of Egypt in the sight of the heathen, that I might be their God: I am the LORD"* (*Leviticus 26:44-45*).

God did not turn away from Israel forever. He promised to **restore** them. He told them that when they returned to Him, repented and obeyed Him with all their heart and soul, that He would have compassion and restore them.

God promised to gather them back from the nations and restore them in their own land:

"Then they will know that I am the LORD their God, for though I sent them into exile among the nations, I will gather them to their own land, not leaving any behind. I

will no longer hide my face from them, for I will pour out my Spirit on the house of Israel, declares the Sovereign LORD" (Ezekiel 39:28-29, NIV).

"And the LORD thy God will bring thee into the land which thy fathers possessed, and thou shalt possess it; and he will do thee good, and multiply thee above thy fathers" (Deuteronomy 30:5).

The establishment of Israel as a nation in 1948 marked the beginning of the restoration of Israel.

God promised to **restore** and prosper their land: *"But ye, O mountains of Israel, ye shall shoot forth your branches, and yield your fruit to my people of Israel; for they are at hand to come. For, behold, I am for you, and I will turn unto you, and ye shall be tilled and sown" (Ezekiel 36:8-9).*

*And I will **restore** to you the years that the locust hath eaten, the cankerworm, and the caterpillar, and the palmerworm, my great army which I sent among you" (Joel 2:25).*

The Hebrew word for "restore" is "Shalam," which means "to give again, make good, repay, recompense." God promised Israel that He would **restore**...repay...recompense Israel all the years the land was made barren and desolate because of their disobedience.

He promised: *"And the desolate land shall be tilled, whereas it lay desolate in the sight of all that passed by. And they shall say, This land that was desolate is become like the garden of Eden; and the waste and desolate and ruined cities are become fenced, and are inhabited" (Ezekiel 36:34-35).*

These promises concerning the restoration of the land have been fulfilled. The land of Israel is *"blossoming as a rose" (Isaiah 35:1).* The land has become fruitful once again.

God promised that the waste places would be built:

"And they shall build the old wastes, they shall raise up the former desolations, and they shall repair the waste cities, the desolations of many generations" (Isaiah 61:4).

*"And I will multiply men upon you, all the house of Israel, even all of it: and the cities shall be inhabited, **and the wastes** shall be builded: And I will multiply upon you man and beast; and they shall increase and bring fruit: and I will settle you after your old estates, and will do better unto*

*you than at your beginnings: and ye shall know that I am
the LORD" (Ezekiel 36:10-11).*

These promises have been fulfilled!

Today as you travel throughout Israel, you will see the
places which once lay in ruins are now rebuilt.

**God promised to gather the Jews from the nations
of the earth and bring them back to Israel:**

... *"but they will say, 'as surely as the LORD lives, who
brought the Israelites up out of the land of the north and out
of all the countries where he had banished them,' For I will
restore them to the land I gave their forefathers" (Jeremiah
16:14-15, NIV).*

*"And I will gather the remnant of my flock out of all the
countries whither I have driven them, and will bring them
again to their folds; and they shall be fruitful and increase"
(Jeremiah 23:3).*

*"Lift up thine eyes round about, and behold: all these
gather themselves together, and come to thee. As I live, saith
the LORD, thou shalt surely clothe thee with them all, as
with an ornament, and bind them on thee, as a bride doeth.
For thy waste and thy desolate places, and the land of thy
destruction, shall even now be too narrow by reason of the
inhabitants, and they that swallowed thee up shall be far
away" (Isaiah 49:18-19).*

We are seeing this restoration taking place today! Three
million Jews from among the nations of the world have returned to Israel. Last year over 50,000 Jews were released
from Russia to return to Israel. With the recent dramatic
changes in the Eastern bloc opening new doors of freedom,
the way has been opened for more to make the exodus.

El Al Airlines has now started making two flights daily
from Moscow to Tel Aviv, taking Jews from Russia to Israel.
Israel's leaders expect to receive 100,000 soviet Jews in the
next three years. I believe that number will be much
higher...as many as 200,000! In Hungary, there has been a
restoration of full diplomatic relations between Hungary
and Israel opening the way for more than 80,000 Jews to
return to Israel.

God promised to restore prosperity to Israel:

"And the LORD thy God will make thee plenteous in every

work of thine hand, in the fruit of thy body, and in the fruit of thy cattle, and in the fruit of thy land, for good: for the LORD will again rejoice over thee for good, as he rejoiced over thy fathers" (Deuteronomy 30:9).

"...Behold, I will send you corn, and wine, and oil, and ye shall be satisfied therewith, and I will no more make you a reproach among the heathen" (Joel 2:19).

"And the floors shall be full of wheat, and the vats shall overflow with wine and oil. **And ye shall eat in plenty, and be satisfied***, and praise the name of the LORD your God, that hath dealt wondrously with you: and my people shall never be ashamed" (Joel 2:24,26).*

"And I will gather the remnant of my flock out of all countries whither I have driven them, and will bring them again to their folds; and they shall be fruitful and increase. And I will set up shepherds over them which shall feed them: **and they shall fear no more, nor be dismayed, neither shall they be lacking, saith the LORD** *" (Jeremiah 23:3-4).*

God promised to restore health:

"For I will restore health unto thee, and I will heal thee of thy wounds, saith the LORD, because they called thee an Outcast, saying, This is Zion, whom no man seeketh after" (Jeremiah 30:17).

God promised to deliver Israel out of the hands of their enemies and restore their position of power and authority over their enemies:

"But thus saith the LORD, Even the captives of the mighty shall be taken away, and the prey of the terrible shall be delivered; for I will contend with him that contendeth with thee, and I will save thy children" (Isaiah 49:25)

"And it shall come to pass in that day, that I will seek to destroy all the nations that come against Jerusalem" (Zechariah 12:9).

"In righteousness shalt thou be established: thou shalt be far from oppression; for thou shalt not fear: and from terror; for it shall not come near thee" (Isaiah 54:14).

As the nation of Israel returns to God with their whole heart and walks in obedience to Him, He is going to bring them together. They are going to be joined together with the Gentiles into one Body. Jesus said, *"There shall be one fold, and one shepherd" (John 10:16).* We are going to serve God together as joint heirs of a new nation...God's spiritual Israel...the Kingdom of God!

"...and they shall be safe in their land, and shall know that I am the LORD, when I have broken the bands of their yoke, and delivered them out of the hand of those that served themselves of them. And they shall no more be a prey to the heathen..." (Ezekiel 34:27-28).

God promised to cleanse Israel from its sins:

A spiritual blindness has been upon the Jews for thousands of years. Paul said, *"God hath given them the spirit of slumber, eyes that they should not see, and ears that they should not hear unto this day (Romans 11:7-8).*

When the "fullness of the Gentiles" has been accomplished, God will remove their blindness and there will be a great wave of salvation and multitudes of Jews will turn to the Lord and be saved.

Paul told the Romans: *"For I would not, brethren, that ye should be ignorant of this mystery, lest ye should be wise in your own conceits; that blindness in part is happened to Israel, **until the fulness of the Gentiles be come in**" (Romans 11:25).*

This is God's hour to open the spiritual eyes of the Jews and open the wells of salvation.

God has promised: *"In that day there shall be a fountain opened to the house of David and to the inhabitants of Jerusalem for sin and for uncleanness" (Zechariah 13:1).*

"And I will cleanse them from all their iniquity, whereby they have sinned against me; and I will pardon all their iniquities, whereby they have sinned, and whereby they have transgressed against me" (Jeremiah 33:8).

"Then will I sprinkle clean water upon you, and ye shall be clean: from all your filthiness, and from all your idols, will I cleanse you, A new heart also will I give you, and a new spirit will I put within you: and I will take away the stony heart out of your flesh, and I will give you an heart of flesh. And I will put my spirit within you, and cause you to walk in my statutes, and ye shall keep my judgments, and do them" (Ezekiel 36:25-27).

We are living in a day of restoration! God is going to restore to Israel everything they lost as a result of their disobedience. Many of these prophecies have been fulfilled. Others we are seeing fulfilled before our eyes. During this time of restoration, all of the promises God has made will be fulfilled.

However, this restoration will not be automatic! Restoration will come to Israel as they repent and turn back to God: All of these blessings will come upon them if they are willing to humble themselves and follow God with their whole heart.

"If thou shalt hearken unto the voice of the LORD thy God, to keep his commandments and his statutes which are written in this book of the law, and if thou turn unto the LORD thy God with all thine heart, and with all thine soul." (Deuteronomy 30:10).

God appeared to Solomon and said: *"If I shut up heaven that there be no rain, or if I command the locusts to devour the land, or if I send pestilence among my people; If my people, which are called by my name, shall humble themselves, and pray, and seek my face, and turn from their wicked ways;* then *will I hear from heaven, and will forgive their sin, and will heal their land"* (II Chronicles 7:13-14).

Before God promised to bring restoration to Israel, He called the priests first, then all the people to repentance.

God said, *"Gird yourselves, and lament, ye priests: howl, ye ministers of the altar: come, lie all night in sackcloth, ye ministers of my God:"* (Joel 1:13).

He told them, *"Sanctify ye a fast, call a solemn assembly, gather the elders and all the inhabitants of the land into the house of the LORD your God, and cry unto the LORD"* (Joel 1:14).

He said, *"Turn ye even to me with all your heart, and with fasting, and with weeping, and with mourning: And rend your heart, and not your garments, and turn unto the LORD your God"* (Joel 2:12-13).

After true repentance...after humbling themselves... after turning away from their wicked ways...after crying out to God...God promised this great restoration would come. He said, ***"Then** will the LORD be jealous for his land, and pity his people"* (Joel 2:18). Then He will drive away their enemies...then His blessings and abundance will flow...

then will He restore the years of famine, drought and adversity!

Israel will be fully restored in every area until it is once again established in its position of power and glory...above all the other nations of the earth. God's power and glory will again be upon Israel and flow through it.

The Body Of Christ Will Be Restored To The Same Power And Authority As Christ!

Just as sure as we see this restoration taking place in Israel, in this decade of the nineties during this coming Wave of Restitution and Restoration, the Body of Christ will experience total restoration in every aspect until we have reached the position of power and authority God has intended for us!

God's plan has always been to have a people who had power and authority upon the earth. When He created Adam and Eve, He created them in His own image and gave them power, authority and dominion to rule upon this earth. He told them, *"Be fruitful and multiply, and replenish the earth, and subdue it: and have domin-ion over the fish of the sea, and over the fowl of the air, and over every living thing that moveth upon the earth"* *(Genesis 1:28)*.

He raised up Israel as His chosen people and gave them power, authority and dominion over all the nations. He promised to set them on high above all nations of the earth.

His plan and purpose was to establish them as a mighty people through whom He would establish His kingdom upon the earth. As long as they would love and obey His commandments, God promised to give them power, authority and dominion...to subdue...conquer...tread down all their enemies. He gave them the land and told them to drive out their enemies. He told Moses, *"Speak unto the children of Israel, and say unto them, When ye are passed over Jordan into the land of Canaan, Then ye shall drive out all the inhabitants of the land from before you"* *(Numbers 33:51-52)*.

God promised Israel: *"The LORD shall cause thine ene-mies that rise up against thee to be smitten before thy face:*

they shall come out against thee one way, and flee before thee seven ways" (Deuteronomy 28:7).

As long as they walked in obedience to God, they were invincible and immovable. All the nations feared them.

God sent Jesus to earth and gave Him power, authority and dominion. He was anointed with the Holy Ghost and with power to destroy the works of the devil. *"God anointed Jesus of Nazareth with the Holy Ghost and with power: who went about doing good, and healing all that were oppressed of the devil; for God was with him" (Acts 10:38).*

Jesus had power, authority and dominion over sin!

Jesus had power, authority and dominion over sickness!

Jesus had power, authority and dominion over all the power of Satan!

Jesus had power, authority and dominion over death!

Jesus gave His twelve disciples power and authority. *"And when he had called unto him his twelve disciples, he gave them power against unclean spirits, to cast them out, and to heal all manner of disease" (Matthew 10:1).* He raised up seventy disciples and gave them the same power and authority (Luke 10:9,17). He told them, *"Behold, I give unto you power to tread on serpents and scorpions, and* **over all the power of the enemy**: *and nothing shall by any means hurt you" (Luke 10:19).*

God, through Christ, has restored and elevated us to a position of power and authority over **all** principalities and powers. When Christ ascended into heaven, He was given a position of supreme power and authority... *"Far above all principality, and power, and might, and dominion, and every name that is named, not only in this world, but also in that which is to come; And hath put all things under his feet" (Ephesians 1:21-22).*

In this position, Christ has established His Church and has given us the same power, authority and dominion.

Christ told Peter, *"...upon this rock I will build my church;* **and the gates of hell shall not prevail against it**" *(Matthew 16:18).*

He has given us the keys to the kingdom of heaven and has promised whatever we bind on earth will be bound in heaven and whatever we loose on earth shall be loosed in heaven! (Matthew 16:19).

Through the power and authority of the Holy Spirit:
- We have power, authority and dominion over sin!
- We have power, authority and dominion over sickness!
- We have power, authority and dominion over all the power of Satan!

The Church has not taken its position of power and authority. We have allowed Satan and his demon principalities to have dominion over our communities, our states, and our countries. We have allowed him to put sickness and disease upon our bodies and upon our loved ones. We have allowed him to hinder the work of the ministry. We have allowed him to bind our finances.

Satan has not stolen our power and authority from us. He doesn't have the power! Just as he didn't have the power to make Adam and Eve sin or to take their position of power and authority over the world, he does not have power to take it from us. The only way he can get it is when we surrender it to him. He gains it by default!

Just as God elevated Israel and set them in a position of power and authority above the nations of the earth, He has established the Body of Christ in a position of power and authority over the earth.

Just as God gave Israel the promised land and told them to drive out their enemies and take possession of it, God has given us the land and through the power of the Holy Spirit we must drive out the enemy and take possession of it!

Through Christ, we have been restored to the position of power, authority and dominion Adam had over the earth. God has given it to us. Now it is up to us to subdue and take dominion over it. The Hebrew root word for "subdue" is "kabash," which means "to trample underfoot...to conquer." The word "dominion" in Hebrew is "radah," which means "to rule over."

In this Wave of Restitution and Restoration that is coming, the Spirit of God will move within the Body of Christ and enable us to rise up in our position of power and authority to trample underfoot...conquer...and drive out Satan and his principalities.

King David said to God: *"Through thee will we push down our enemies: through thy name will we tread them under that rise up against us" (Psalm 44:5).* No longer will the Church run and hide. No longer will we sit back and allow Satan and his demon principalities to exercise dominion over our loved ones...over our cities... over our nations! No longer will we stay on the defensive, where we are waiting for the enemy to attack us.

Restoration is coming to the Body of Christ in every aspect of our lives until we have been perfected into the same image of Jesus Christ, where we are a representation and manifestation of all that Christ is!

We will rise up with the same power and authority of Jesus Christ. In His power and in His Name, we will go forth on the job...in our homes...in our cities...in our nations...and we will push down and tread upon our enemies. In this coming major Crisis of Satanic Confrontation, we will not be intimidated, but we will face Satan and his demon principalities...not in our own power...but in the same power and authority as Jesus.

In your life, how has the enemy been coming against you...in your physical body...in your mind...in your finances...in your relationships? Christ has restored you to a position of power and authority. Just as God promised Israel, *"The Lord shall cause thine enemies that rise up against thee to be smitten before thy face: they shall come out against thee one way, and flee before thee seven ways" (Deuteronomy 28:7),* as you go forward in Christ's power and authority, Satan and his demon principalities are going to be defeated before you. They are going to come against you one way, but they will flee from you seven ways!

What are the areas in your life where Satan has attacked and tried to destroy you? He may have attacked you in your marriage and it seems there is no hope. It may be that Satan has been oppressing you in your mind until you feel discouraged, defeated and ready to give up. He may have come against you and attacked your finances until you are at a loss to know what to do. Physically, Satan may have brought sickness and disease upon your body, or you may be under such stress on your job that you feel you cannot take any more and are ready to give up.

Just as God promised to restore and build up the waste places in the nation of Israel, during this time of restoration, He will restore the "waste places" in your life. Just as God promised Israel to restore "the years that the locust hath eaten," He will restore the years the enemy has wreaked havoc in your life...the years of heartache, anguish, sorrow...the years of discouragement and defeat...the years of pain...the years of poverty and want.

What are the waste places in your life?

Through Christ, you have been restored in every aspect of your life. In this Wave of Restitution and Restoration, you must take your position of power and authority to drive out the enemy and take back the territory that belongs to you...healing...a 100 percent free and healthy mind...a happy marriage...God's supernatural provision in your life...everything that belongs to you as a child of the living God!

We have been restored to the total wholeness...spirit, soul and body...that is in Christ. God created Adam and Eve after His own image. They were a representation and manifestation of God. Their hearts and minds were 100 percent healthy and free from all contamination. They possessed the ability to rule over every aspect of their minds...their thoughts...imaginations...emotions...and will. Their spirits, souls, and bodies were in perfect harmony with God.

When they surrendered their wills to Satan, they lost the ability to rule over their minds...wills...thoughts...imaginations. Instead of their spirits, souls and bodies functioning together in perfect harmony with God, their minds were under the dominion and control of Satan and their carnal minds ruled over their spirits and bodies.

Through Christ, we have been restored and it is possible for us to have the 100 percent victorious mind of Christ. God's purpose for us during this time of restoration is that we be conformed and transformed into the same image of Christ, where Christ in all His fullness is manifested in our innermost being. He plans for you to have the same powerful, 100 percent victorious mind of Christ operating in your life.

Paul told the Corinthians: *"For who has known or understood the mind (the counsels and purposes) of the Lord so as to guide and instruct (Him) and give Him knowledge?* But we have the mind of Christ, *the Messiah, and do hold the thoughts (feelings and purposes) of His heart"* (I Corinthians 2:16, TAB).

The "mind" of Christ is His thoughts, His will, His purposes. It is referring to the vast depth of the riches in both the wisdom and knowledge of God...His judgments.

God has revealed the "mind of Christ" to us through His Word. As we fill our hearts and minds with His Word, and bring our minds into submission to His thoughts, His will, His purposes, His desires, we are transformed into His image...we have His mind, and we are able to walk in power and victory over all the power of the enemy.

Through the power of the Holy Spirit within you, you are able to take authority over every carnal thought, every carnal desire, every temptation of the flesh, and bring it into line with the Word of God. You have the power to have the 100 percent victorious mind of Christ, but God expects you to exercise your power and authority over your carnal mind to take possession of it.

What are the areas in your mind over which you have allowed Satan to exercise dominion?

You have been restored and through Christ you have the power to bring every aspect of your mind...your thoughts...imaginations...emotions and will into harmony with God. There is no reason why your mind should be filled with worry, fear, doubt and unbelief. There is no reason your mind should be so weighted down with the cares of this life that you are stressed out and unable to cope with the problems you are facing. There is no reason your mind should be filled with negative thoughts, impure, unholy desires.

In this time of restoration that is coming, God wants you to exercise your power and authority in the areas of your mind, where Satan has built strongholds, and drive him out! By faith, you must take possession of the 100 percent restored mind Christ has made possible for you to have.

In this Wave of Restitution and Restoration that is coming

to the Body of Christ, we will experience restoration in our families. In the midst of the turmoil and problems we will face in the Crisis of the Family that God has revealed to us is coming, we will also experience restoration!

Just as God promised Israel, *"I will contend with him that contendeth with thee, and **I will save thy children**"* *(Isaiah 49:25),* He will save and deliver our children and loved ones. The word "save" translated from the original Hebrew means "defend, deliver, preserve, bring total salvation...mind, body, soul and spirit."

During this time of restoration before Christ's return, there will be a wave of salvation that will come, where many of our unsaved children and loved ones for whom we have been praying, believing and holding onto God many years for their deliverance and salvation, will be saved.

As the Body of Christ rises up in the power and authority Christ has given us over Satan and his principalities, we will break his bondage in the lives of our loved ones and **drive** him out.

The power of God will be released through us as we come together in times of prayer and fasting on behalf of our unsaved children and loved ones. We will experience a new boldness as we speak the Word and warn of the judgments of God that are coming upon the earth and of Christ's soon return.

Unsaved members of our families we have agonized over for years and years will suddenly become receptive to the Word of God and will turn to God. When they see the great crises that are coming upon the earth, they will come to us looking for the solutions to their problems.

What are the waste places in your family...the areas where you have allowed Satan to exercise dominion? What are the areas in your family where he has entered in and destroyed? There may be broken relationships between family members. Your marriage may be falling apart. You may have rebellious teenagers who are running from God or who are bound by drugs or alcohol.

God has promised restoration! He has promised to build up the "waste places." Take the power and authority Christ has given you and drive out the enemy!

Wave 5: Restitution and Restoration For The Church!

When God created Adam and Eve and placed them in the Garden of Eden, they were perfectly whole in every way. They had no physical defects, disabilities or limitations. God never intended for man to experience pain, sickness or death.

Man lost this perfect health when Adam and Eve rebelled and surrendered their wills to Satan. Sin, sickness and death came upon the earth as a result of the curse. Until the curse is totally removed from the earth, when God creates a new heaven and a new earth (Revelation 22:3), man will be susceptible to Satan's attacks of sickness and disease upon their bodies. However, God has restored divine health to us in the Name of Jesus!

When God delivered Israel (approximately 2.5 million Jews) out of Egyptian bondage, there was not one feeble person among them: *"And he brought forth his people with joy, and his chosen with gladness: And gave them the lands of the heathen: and they inherited the labor of the people...He brought them forth also with silver and gold: **and there was not one feeble person among their tribes***" (Psalm 105:43-44,37).

He promised them, *"And the LORD will take away from thee all sickness, and will put none of the evil diseases of Egypt which thou knowest, upon thee"* (Deuteronomy 7:15). Even after they turned their backs upon Him and reaped the curses which included sickness and disease (Deuteronomy 28:59-61), God promised to restore their health. He said, *"I will restore health unto thee, and I will heal thee of thy wounds"* (Jeremiah 30:17).

Jesus came to earth to destroy the works of the devil...to break the power of sin, sickness and death. God gave Him power, authority and dominion over sickness and He healed all those who were oppressed of the devil.

*"...God anointed Jesus of Nazareth with the Holy Ghost and with power: who went about doing good, **and healing all that were oppressed of the devil; for God was with him**"* (Acts 10:38).

While He was still upon the earth, Jesus gave His disciples power and authority over sickness. *"And when he had called unto him his twelve disciples, he gave them power against un-*

*clean spirits, to cast them out, **and to heal all manner of sickness and all manner of disease** " (Matthew 10:1).*

When He sent the 70 disciples out, He gave them power and authority over sickness. He commanded them *"...into whatsoever city ye enter, and they receive you, eat such things as are set before you: **And heal the sick that are therein**, and say unto them, The kingdom of God is come nigh unto you" (Luke 10:8-9).*

Jesus has given us the **same** power and authority over sickness and disease! Before He ascended into heaven, Jesus said, *"And these signs shall follow them that believe...they shall lay hands on the sick, and they shall recover" (Mark 16:17-18).*

Christ has restored us to total wholeness...spirit, soul and body. Through the Holy Spirit within us, we have power and authority over sickness and disease. God has made it possible for us to live in divine health. When Satan tries to put sickness upon us, we have the power and authority to drive him out and take the healing Christ has provided for us.

In this time of restoration, a Wave of Healing is going to sweep through the Body of Christ. We will rise up in the power and authority Christ has given us to take the healing that belongs to us and to lay hands on the sick. We will walk in divine health. That does not mean that Satan won't try to afflict our bodies with sickness and disease, but that when he does, we will use the power and authority Christ has given us to rebuke the sickness and command it to leave in the Name of Jesus, and it will go!

You have been restored to the total wholeness that is in Christ! What are the areas in your physical body where you have allowed Satan to exercise dominion and afflict your body? Whatever the sickness or disease you may have afflicting your body right now, rise up in faith. Lay your hand on the part of your body that is afflicted and in the Name of Jesus rebuke the affliction and command it to go. Take back the divine health Christ has restored to you. Do not listen to Satan's lies one minute longer. Refuse to let go of God's promises of healing; persevere in faith until you receive your healing!

Drive The Enemy Out Of Your Finances And Take Possession Of God's Blessings Of Prosperity!

Just as God has promised to restore prosperity to Israel, during the coming wave of Restitution and Restoration, God will restore our finances so that we will have His supernatural provision in our lives.

God's promise to Israel is: *"...I will restore to you the years that the locust hath eaten..." (Joel 2:25).*

"Bring ye all the tithes into the storehouse, that there may be meat in mine house, and prove me now herewith, saith the LORD of hosts, if I will not open you the windows of heaven, and pour you out a blessing, that there shall not be room enough to receive it" (Malachi 3:10).

He said *"And I will rebuke the devourer for your sakes, and he shall not destroy the fruits of your ground..." (Malachi 3:11).*

During this time of Israel's restoration, God has promised: *"And the floors shall be full of wheat, and the vats shall overflow with wine and oil. And ye shall eat in **plenty, and be satisfied** ..." (Joel 2:24,26).*

God's plan and purpose has always been to bless and prosper His people. When He delivered them out of Egyptian bondage, He gave them the spoils of Egypt. As He was bringing them into the promised land, He promised to bring them into a land where there would be no shortage of food and they would lack nothing (Deuteronomy 8:9). Even after they forfeited His blessings of prosperity because of their disobedience and rebellion, God promised, *"And they shall fear no more, nor be dismayed, **neither shall they be lacking**, saith the LORD" (Jeremiah 23:4).*

In the early Church, God supernaturally provided for His people. *"**Neither was there any among them that lacked**" (Acts 4:34).*

Through Christ, we have been **restored** to a position where God's blessings of prosperity are upon us. This is not the prosperity according to the world's standards, but the supernatural provision of God where our needs are met and there is no lack!

In the coming worldwide financial crisis, God's hand of

supernatural provision will be seen upon His people. It will not be the absence of problems and adversity among God's people that will be a witness to the world, but in the midst of this financial crisis the world will see God's strong arm of provision for His people.

God's promise to us today is: *"And ye shall eat in plenty, and be satisfied" (Joel 2:26)*. His plan is that all the needs in your life will be met. As we keep our covenant with God and are faithful and obedient to His Word in paying our vows and giving our tithes and offerings, we can expect God's supernatural provision in our lives. He has promised, *"Call on Me in the day of trouble; I will deliver you, and you shall honor and glorify Me" (Psalm 50:15, TAB)*.

God has said that in times of trouble…in the midst of the financial difficulties…in the midst of the coming crises…in perilous times…"I will deliver you!" God's plan of restoration for the Body of Christ today is that we be satisfied… that we do not go lacking!

You have been restored to total wholeness in Christ! What are the "waste places" in the area of your finances that need to be restored? You may be facing severe financial difficulties, where you are unable to pay outstanding bills. There may be pressing needs in your family and you do not have the finances to meet those needs.

Whatever the financial needs you are facing right now in your life, by faith take the power and authority Christ has given you, bind Satan and the principalities that are binding and attacking your finances and **drive** them out. Take possession of God's blessings of prosperity. Look to Him and receive His supernatural provision for all your needs

Just as all God's promises concerning restoration will be fulfilled until Israel is fully restored in every area, during this Wave of Restitution and Restoration, the Body of Christ will experience full restoration until we are restored to the total wholeness…spirit, soul, body…that has been made possible through Christ.

Go Forward In This Decade Of Spiritual Destiny Fully Prepared And Equipped To Be 100 Percent Victorious!

I have revealed to you the Five Major Crises and the Five

Wave 5: Restitution and Restoration For The Church!

Major Waves of the Spirit that God has shown me are coming in this last decade of the century:

Five Major Crises:

Crisis 1: **A Crisis of Change**

Crisis 2: **Crisis of the Family**

Crisis 3: **Crisis of the Church**

Crisis 4: **A Major Worldwide Financial Crisis**

Crisis 5: **A Crisis of Satanic Confrontation**

Five Major Waves Of The Holy Spirit:

A Wave of **True Holiness**

A Wave of **Signs, Wonders and Miracles**

A Wave of **True Unity**

A Wave of **Wisdom and Discernment**

A Wave of **Restitution and Restoration**

God has made you part of His endtime Spiritual Destiny. This Decade of Spiritual Destiny will be...

A time of fulfillment of God's plan and purpose for man!

A time of manifestation...where there is a full manifestation of God's power flowing through the true Body of Christ!

A time of consummation...where God is bringing all things together and heading them up in Christ.

A time of demonstration of the miracle power of God as a final endtime witness to the world.

A time of final preparation...where the Body of Christ is preparing itself for the coming of Christ.

Take your position as part of God's people of destiny!

Set a watch in prayer!

Go forward in this decade with...

• A New Authority
• A New Boldness
• A New Fearlessness
• A Divine Capability

...to fulfill His purposes upon the earth!

Take your position of power and authority where you are being transformed into the same image of Christ, where you are a visible representation and manifestation of Christ in the fullness of His Being!

You Need To Be Prepared!

Now you can know the prophetic events, happening now – and yet to come…By joining God's Victorious Army!

God's Victorious Army…

The largest, most advanced thrust of God in the Body of Christ today Now you and your family can be prepared to withstand the onslaught of Satan in this endtime hour.

Now you can know God's divine will for this hour! God's Victorious Army is a unique band of men and women from all walks of life who have the power of God manifested in their lives for VICTORY in every situation.

GVA is people like you... is people like you...who have a desire to see souls won for the Kingdom of God. Membership in GVA sponsors our training of third world National ministers, teaching them how to preach the Gospel with miracles and signs following as mass evangelists, crusades...the only way to reach the world for Jesus Christ before His soon return!
And, you will be **trained, strengthened, equipped** and **prepared**...

You will experience **victory** in every area of your life!
You will overcome **every** attack of the enemy!
You will **know** the prophetic
events in this endtime hour!

Each month you will receive...

A 48-page workbook-style manual that gives you the keys to victory and peace for your life and the lives of your loved ones. You will be strengthened...you will learn how to have the joy of Victory in your life by overcoming all circumstances
And, you will learn to work the works of God and see the

spiritual power of God move in behalf of your life just like thousands of men and women have all over the world.
Right now, join God's Victorious Army by checking the box on the coupon in the back of this book. Be sure to enclosed your first month's gift of $20 or more with the coupon.

God has a miracle for you!

But first you must act.! Sign up for God's Victorious Army right now...and we will rush you your first Victory Miracle Library Lesson, your membership card and beautiful lapel pin!

Get ready – your life will never be the same!

New! First time offered!

Global Prophecy In Action

A prophetic newsletter that tracks world-wide events manifesting the Five Waves of the Holy Spirit and the Five Major Crisis now unfolding in this decade of destiny

Each month, you will receive...

- **Up to the minute** on prophetic events unfolding around the globe.
- **Prophecy warnings** concerning events that can effect your life.
- **Your prophecy questions** will be personally answered in a unique, unprecedented, question and answer format.
- *Prophecy In Action* will demonstrate to you its on time manifestation of the prophecies God has given His servant, Morris Cerullo.
- *Prophecy In Action* will tell you what your next move should be as you prepare for God's endtime manifesta tions, and the soon-coming of Jesus Christ.
- **Special prophetic books** will be offered to you first in this newsletter.

Global Prophecy In Action follows the prophetic events vital to you as a Christian, and helps you understand God's divine purpose in this endtime hour.

Don't miss a single issue.

Order yours today by completing the coupon on the back of this page.

Dear Brother Cerullo,

☐ Please enroll me in God's Victorious Army.
I want to receive the forty-eight page, monthly Victory Miracle Library Lessons — and be TRAINED, STRENGTHENED, and PREPARED in these endtimes. I will join in monthly support to train third world Nationals for this vital endtime ministry.
You can count on me to send monthly:

☐ $20   ☐ $25   ☐ $50   ☐ $(£)_____
   (£10)   (£15)   (£25)

Place here the amount the Holy Spirit leads you to commit.

☐ Here is my gift of love to support this ministry:

$(£)_____. Please send me your new prophecy newsletter, "Global Prophecy In Action."

Name

Address

City

State or Province

Zip or Postal Code   Telephone

Area Code

Mail back today to:

Morris Cerullo World Evangelism
P.O. Box 85277 • San Diego, CA 92186

Morris Cerullo World Evangelism of Canada
P.O. Box 2555, Station C • Downsview, Ontario M3N 2Y1

Morris Cerullo World Evangelism
P.O. Box 277 • Hemel Hempstead, Herts HP2 7DH